DRIVEN

DRIVEN

A WHITE-KNUCKLED RIDE TO HEARTBREAK AND BACK

A Memoir

Melissa Stephenson

Houghton Mifflin Harcourt

Boston   New York

2018

For information about permission to reproduce selections
from this book, write to trade.permissions@hmhco.com or to
Permissions, Houghton Mifflin Harcourt Publishing Company,
3 Park Avenue, 19th Floor, New York, New York 10016.

hmhco.com

Library of Congress Cataloging-in-Publication Data
Names: Stephenson, Melissa, author.
Title: Driven : a white-knuckled ride to heartbreak and back / Melissa
Stephenson. Description: Boston : Houghton Mifflin Harcourt, 2018. |
Identifiers: LCCN 2018009677 (print) | LCCN 2017045349 (ebook) |
ISBN 9781328768308 (ebook) | ISBN 9781328768292 (hardback)
Subjects: LCSH: Stephenson, Melissa (Creative Writer). | Automobile
travel — United States. | Automobiles — Social aspects — United States. |
Automobile driving — United States — Psychological aspects. |
Middle West — Biography | Women — Middle West — Biography. |
BISAC: BIOGRAPHY & AUTOBIOGRAPHY / Personal Memoirs. |
FAMILY & RELATIONSHIPS / Siblings. | FAMILY & RELATION-
SHIPS / Death, Grief, Bereavement. | TRANSPORTATION /
Automotive / General. | TRAVEL / United States / Midwest / General. |
Classification: LCC CT275.S68725 (print) |
LCC CT275.S68725 A3 2018 (ebook) | DDC 305.40977 — DC23
LC record available at https://lccn.loc.gov/2018009677

Book design by Chrissy Kurpeski
Typeset in Chronicle Text

Printed in the United States of America
DOC 10 9 8 7 6 5 4 3 2 1

for Matthew

When everything seems to be going against you, remember that the airplane takes off against the wind, not with it.

— HENRY FORD

Prologue

Texas: August 2000

*F*IVE ON FRIDAY DURING rush hour in a city and state both new to me, and my dead brother's truck starts honking its horn, loud and aggressive as gunfire. *Honk honk honk.* The truck has no air conditioning and the tweed upholstery feels both slick and scratchy against the damp backs of my legs. I'm on an access road that flanks the interstate, following an inside lane to where it U-turns at the underpass. I feel like a rodent lost in a closed-circuit maze. As I turn toward my side of the highway, the horn blares again. *Honk. Honk. HONK.* I have no choice but to keep going, a road hazard in a red '79 Ford F-150 with Confederate flag plates. This truck, it seems, is driving me.

One guy flips me the bird. Others stare. Some throw their hands up in confusion. Those who get a good look discover a hundred-pound white girl with a ballerina's neck and an arm full of tattoos behind the wheel, shocked beyond tears. I cross into the far right lane so I can pull over before I get my ass kicked. Each time the horn honks, I feel my brother is fucking with me for making off with his ride. The honking seems to be growing louder, though I know that's not possible. *Honk HONK HONK.* I coast into a spot near some trees at the edge of a Kentucky Fried Chicken parking lot and cut the engine. The chaos ends as suddenly as it began, and for a moment my whole being feels like the still space between heartbeats: body buzzing, ears deaf with silence, the world arrested. *Is this what it feels like,* I wonder, *to be dead?*

I sit, waiting for my next move to announce itself. The thought of having the truck towed because of a horn glitch is beyond embarrassing. My husband knows far less about cars than I do, so there's no point in calling him. I search the cab as if I might find a solution in an object. The console holds a half-pack of my brother's smokes, a collection of mix tapes (some I made for him), matchbooks, and spare change. I light a cigarette and assess my predicament.

Two weeks ago, my new husband and I left our home in Montana for Texas, a move I regret already. My brother died suddenly six days ago, after we arrived in San Marcos, where our zip code ends in 666. Now I'm stranded in a KFC parking lot as the temperature climbs above 110. My new driver's license is nothing but a piece of paper folded inside my wallet — temporary, a placeholder. And this truck? I don't even know the dimensions of the thing. I could walk home, but my gut says this is the kind of truck someone might steal. It has little orange running lights on top, a fresh red paint job, a corrugated steel toolbox, and the sort of after-market steering wheel you'd find on a racecar. I don't dare abandon my only sibling's prized possession, left to me by default.

I close my eyes and focus. (Grief has overwhelmed my systems — I can now experience the full range of human emotion in minutes, but logic comes slowly, like reciting the alphabet backwards.) The heat amplifies in the stillness. *What would Matthew do?*

The toolbox.

I climb into the truck bed and unlock the steel box with the smaller of the two keys. Inside: my brother's tools, a pair of leather work gloves, and a repair manual. Though I'm wearing only Converse, cutoffs, and a black tank-top (Texas has already cured me of the need for undergarments), the sun sears my back with such intensity that sweat drips down my chest, my sides, slides off my chin and splatters on the manual.

I gather up my findings, unlatch the hood, and stare down the giant six-cylinder engine. All my cars so far have been four cylinders and fuel-injected, not carbureted like this one. To get a better look, I climb into the engine compartment and perch myself on the edge of the body.

Think.

Wires and a fuse control the horn. If the horn can honk, the fuse is good. It has to be a bad wire, something pinched or ungrounded, a loose connection. The horn went off each time I turned. I picture that tiny racing wheel atop a thick steering column, and I know that's gotta be it — the wires crammed like a geisha's foot into a shoe. I open the manual and flip through electrical diagrams. Though I have loved cars my whole life, my experience is in driving them, not fixing them. I haven't done much more than change oil or an occasional tire — even those jobs managed in spite of self-doubt.

Stop it. Just THINK.

I search the index for "horn." If I can find the thing, I can disconnect it, but the diagrams offer no drawing or picture of the actual horn. It's hard to find what you need when you have no idea what it looks like. Though the front of the truck is shaded by a tree at the edge of the lot, I grow hotter and more nauseous by the minute. When Matthew died, so did my appetite. The more I study the diagrams, the less sense they make.

A kind of mental vertigo I am prone to when under pressure takes hold. In my final year of college, a French teacher caught me daydreaming in class and threw chalk at my head to illustrate the meaning of the verb *jeté* ("to throw"), a word I knew inside and out after a decade of ballet lessons and five years of French. But put me in the headlights and I'll go deer on you every time.

Breathe.

I remind myself there is no sweaty man yelling at me in this parking lot. The smell of fried chicken provokes a wave of nausea so intense that I climb off the truck and stand in the grass with my head between my knees. Tears come instead of vomit. My brain gives up on logic, taxed from the brief attempt to fix a simple thing. As reason slips away, my emotions kick into overdrive, and I kick a live oak tree older than me as cars whiz by. A stray customer wanders out of the KFC with a hot bucket under her arm. I kick the tree again, curse, and punch it. The pain in my knuckles turns my rage into shame, and I curl up, knees to chest, back resting against the giant front tire. My throbbing knuckles feel more real than any other part of this new Texas life. I sob till I'm hyperventilating, like I did when I was a child.

The last time I had a public meltdown was a half-decade ago, during college, when my Volkswagen van got the yellow parking boot while I was in class. Turned out I owed $150 in tickets, $150 I didn't have, so I went fetal on the curb and cried. Now I have better reasons for crying — a dead brother, a busted truck, and a cross-country move to hell — but I feel just as stupid as I did when I was four or eighteen.

I focus on breathing. The idea of another cigarette appeals to me, and I open my eyes. On the ground next to my feet are those gloves. His gloves. The leather holds the shape of his hands. I slide them on, one at a time, my fingers so small inside I feel like a child, a forever little sister. *This,* I think, *may be as close to him as I'll ever again get.*

I stand, steadying myself on the Ford as the world wobbles. In spite of the horn, I do the thing I do best, the thing I do every chance I get, the thing I do when all else turns to shit: I fire up that engine and drive.

Part 1

ONE

First Rides

Indiana: 1970s

I'M NOT SURPRISED THAT the only thing of material value my brother left behind was a truck, since I'm pretty sure he was created in the backseat of a car, and my most vivid memories of our childhood are of cars, and him — often in tandem.

My brother and I had in our early days a different kind of love/hate relationship: I loved him and he hated me. But our family came together around cars — objects designed, from top to bottom, to work for you, with you, to complement and propel you. Wheels were a necessity growing up in Indiana — a state most pass through on their way to somewhere else. From the time I remember remembering, I knew you needed a car if you were ever going to get anywhere at all. I bonded with the vehicles of my youth the way some children attached themselves to blankets or stuffed animals. I didn't realize until I was grown and gone that not everyone gets excited at the sight of a popped hood, the flash of chrome trim running the length of a vintage Dodge Dart, or a whiff of the vinyl interior of a Volkswagen Squareback warmed by the sun.

Here is our automotive genealogy, our story.

My father, the oldest of five, hailed from a swath of cornfields off Highway 421 in Boone County, Indiana, just north of Indianapolis. His childhood consisted of farm work and school. He shared a double bed with his brothers, the three of them sleeping head-to-toe until they left home. Dinner leftovers and snack foods didn't exist in that house, though Jesus hung over them in one of those hologram pictures that shifted from crucifixion to headshot as you walked across the living room.

My brother and I loved to hear stories about my father's childhood. He'd tell us how all of his clothes came from the church donation pile. *I'd have to pick someone else's boogers off my high-water corduroys before I wore them,* he'd say. Stories like this made us feel loved and rich by comparison (though we were as far from wealthy as we were from either coast — a fact our parents hid from us by acts of near magic).

How my father ever got enough money to buy the used Chevy he was driving when, at age nineteen, he began courting my mom, I have no idea. Perhaps from several summers spent corn husking on nearby farms? He lost half his left thumb when, as he was riding on a flatbed truck and pulling ears off the stalks, the husking machine snagged his hand. I used to touch that callusy stump, rub it like a talisman, and make him tell me the story again and again: *After it got cut off? I walked home and your Mamaw patched it up. But my friends found the tip and stuck it on top of a stop sign. I saw it on my walk to school the next day. Never occurred to me I should have kept it, that they maybe could have sewed it back on.*

My mother grew up in Lebanon, Indiana — the seat of Boone County. A town girl with a teacher for a mother and a state trooper father, she was the second oldest of four siblings. They lived in a fifties housing development where the kids ran from yard to yard and house to house while the parents socialized over cocktails.

When she was fourteen, getting sent home from school for

wearing a too-short go-go dress was my mother's biggest problem, until the day a semi-truck driver lost consciousness and an-
nihilated her father. He'd been assisting an elderly woman whose
car stranded her on I-65, the main artery that connects Indy and
Chicago. He was killed instantly, honorably, in the line of duty, reduced to a stain on the highway despite his well-known charm and
integrity. He left behind my grandmother and the four children
who called her Betty behind her back and Mother to her face.

I'd make Mom tell me that story over and over as well, wondering how I might feel if anything so spectacular ever marked my
life: *I realized something bad had happened when all of us got called
into the office. We walked home together, and when we saw the police
cars at our house, I remember saying out loud to Bonnie and Lisa,
"God — I hope it's Betty." But it wasn't. It was our dad.*

The next year, my mother's first love, Max, died in a car accident. He'd been both anchor and anesthesia after her father's
death. My father — one of Max's best friends — grieved along with
my mother. My dad was no stranger to tragedy either. The year before, another best friend of his had driven his motorcycle straight
into a construction barrier at high speed one night. *He got his
whole face smashed off,* Dad told me. After the Max accident, Dad
started checking in on my mother, finding the small-town house
run by four teenagers a lively reprieve from his stoic family farm
on State Road 421. My mother was fun, smart, and pretty. Eventually, he made her laugh. They started talking. They went for a drive
— a resilient choice for two kids who'd lost so much to cars already.

Dad says an ex-girlfriend of his painted a sunset on the trunk of
the Chevy one night in secret after he'd started dating my mother.
It was a territorial move — a visual reminder of a previous romance
— but it didn't stop my folks from starting a family in the backseat
of that car, or so Dad hinted more than once. A half-year later, in
1971, my great-grandmother gifted my parents three hundred dol-

lars to purchase a better vehicle. They were by then a pair of long-haired newlyweds renting an apartment in Indianapolis, which brought them a step closer to Bloomington, where my father pursued a degree in social work at Indiana University. Leaving Boone County was not a common or expected move.

It takes a lot of gall, their families said. *It takes a lot of drive.*

When my mom was nine months pregnant, my dad came home one day with a miles-wide grin and a sixties Fiat. Orange. Two doors, with only a whisper of a backseat. The racy little ride was his antidote to matrimony and paternity, perhaps — a nineteen-year-old's attempt at balance. Mom rubbed her belly to reassure her unborn child. "Where is the baby going to ride?"

Dad regarded the car and let loose a nervous laugh — the trademark reaction to confrontation that runs, to this day, the length of the Stephenson family line.

"Give me the keys." She held open her hand.

Barely able to clear the steering wheel with her popped-out navel, she drove the car back to the lot and came home with what should have been a more sensible vehicle: a sedan made by Toyota, a company new to the States. Ads promised buyers would "get their money's worth" on a "car that doesn't ask for much," which would lead them to exclaim, "Oh, what a feeling."

Our mother — a poor, pregnant, fatherless, teenage newlywed — needed the kind of feeling the Toyota promised: security in the form of four doors, a full backseat, and a sticker price she could afford.

Mom gave birth to my brother not long before her eighteenth birthday, and my folks soon moved forty miles south to Columbus, Indiana, where my father took a job at a halfway house while continuing to work on his college degree. Both the Toyota and my brother overwhelmed them with unexpected complications. Dad kept taking the Toyota back to the dealership for repair. Each time he surrendered the car to the shop, he'd have to pedal his ten-speed to the halfway house and bum rides from friends to attend classes in Bloomington. Dad racked up sixty- to eighty-hour weeks between his job and his studies. He worked night shifts and changing hours, often sleeping till noon.

Mom and Matthew spent most days stranded at home, not that she minded. Despite her initial horror at the sight of my brother's forceps-bruised face, she loved her baby dearly. She had good walking shoes and a stroller and kept herself looking nice, skimming magazines in the aisles at the grocery, trying out a new type of braid, an unusual shade of nail polish, her blue eyes thickly lined in black.

Matthew was a difficult baby who cried without pause. In the night. In the day. In the stroller, their bed, his department store crib. But the few moments he calmed and smiled they savored like blue skies in a northern winter. Alert, he'd study their faces: dark hair, bright eyes shiny with hope. They were good-looking people: our mother in the ballpark of a young Cher, our father a dead ringer for Jackson Browne.

It turned out Matthew had colic and an allergy to our mother's milk. Mom gave up breastfeeding for hypoallergenic formula — a change she also says was fine by her, but the medication for Matthew's colic made his teeth crumble not long after they erupted. Until the age of seven, he looked part vampire — nothing in his top jaw between the incisors other than bare, pink gums.

In the year after my brother's birth my folks finagled for themselves a childless vacation, an event that wouldn't occur again until the fall I turned fourteen. I don't know how the idea for a road trip to Arizona came to them, though I bet my father longed to travel a stretch of Route 66 and taste the desert air of the Southwest. Though Dad committed to a life as a family man without hesitation, he's always had a flicker of wanderlust as sure as my mother's love of nesting. I bet my mother agreed to the trip for the thrill of escape, leaving behind laundry, diapers, and sleepless nights to spend an entire week basking in my father's attention.

A few days before they left, my father got up early to tinker with the car. By then, they had traded in the unreliable Toyota for a Ford Galaxy, but the Ford was sprouting a series of ominous symptoms too. Dad told our mother not to worry, that the Ford had issues but he'd saved enough for bus fare back if they had to abandon it. Mom nodded and went on with her day, packing and cleaning and tending to my brother, whom she kept always in range, her nerves tethered to his moods, appetite, and temperature. The next morning, Dad woke to find Mom back from Indianapolis with a Mustang Fastback — a ride fit for Steve McQueen. If my mother was going to spend day after day in a car with her man in the heat of summer, she was going to look good doing it.

With an eight-cylinder engine and the overall weight of a Honda Civic, that late-sixties Mustang could fly. It balanced perfectly my mother's need for function and my father's desire for power. It was also practical enough for a pair of young parents to throw the kids in back and hit the drive-in.

In the single photo of my parents from their trip in the summer of '72, my mother wears a tight white T-shirt with a black peace sign, oversize sunglasses, and cutoff jean shorts with a single inch of inseam, her brown hair parted down the middle, her limbs model-long and tan. My father stands beside her in threadbare flares and a tank-top, hair shaggy to the shoulders, with sideburns and a beard. The desert gapes behind them, wide and alien as a moonscape. Even the stranger snapping the shot must have been smitten with these two humans in full bloom.

I came along in October of 1974 — my conception (as my mother often told me) the result of a negative interaction between her birth control pills and antibiotics. By the time I turned four and my brother seven, our folks bought a white house with brown shutters near a park with a cemetery. Next they found a mate for the Mustang — a '68 Volkswagen Squareback. With two cars, a two-story house, two parents, and two children, we looked like a poster family for the American nuclear unit of 1978. My parents had created the Western dream of success they'd been raised to believe in, a dream so many would find in the eighties — a couple of kids from the boonies do the right thing, work hard, and manage to land a mortgage on a budget slim as a toddler's shoestring.

It was the beginning of a story, no doubt, but not the story we expected. It was the beginning of a story about all the ways the wheels come off.

August 6, 2000

I wonder what memories ran through my brother's mind that last Sunday in Georgia when he was still alive, if any. I've imagined that day for years now, stitching together a story I can understand from the evidence, what his friends said, and memories of the Matthew I knew. A story, in the end, is something more than nothing.

I know this: he never liked Sundays. When we were kids, Sunday meant getting up and getting dressed and trying to sneak candy during the long sermon at our Presbyterian church. Once Matthew grew up, Indiana Sundays meant locked booze coolers and downtown closed up the way real cities do only for Christmas. Once he moved to Georgia, Sundays meant hangovers, a stranger's makeup on his pillowcase, and a day off from his job running garbage with nothing to do but sweat.

As the sun shines through his curtained window the morning of August sixth, heating up the trailer hours before he feels ready to wake, the light tints his closed lids gold and he fights and fights until his head comes alive in spite of him, as dense and unsteady as a sack of wet concrete. He looks at the collection of cups on the bedside table — empty. His head is throbbing now.

He sits up slowly, amazed how many joints in a body can hurt at once. The dog's tail beats joy into the linoleum floor over the sight of him conscious. He thinks about last night, how he was too drunk to bring a girl home, to even remember. He'd hit the bars downtown. Near closing time, he took a rest on a bench and the ground thwacked him awake and he crawled up and rested again.

Now, another Sunday alone with the Quiet.

TWO

The Squarebacks

Indiana: 1975–78

W E WOULD GO THROUGH two Squarebacks — a navy followed by a red. These economy vehicles sparked my lifelong love of Volkswagens. (Volkswagens, like tattoos, build character.) When most people think about early VWs, they picture the Beetle, also known as a Type 1, or the equally celebrated Microbus, a Type 2. The Type 3, sold in the U.S. from '61 through '73, was the third mass-produced VW design. They came in three models: a Notchback sedan, a sporty Fastback, and the Squareback station wagon.

In one television ad for the Squareback, a man unloaded suitcases from the full trunk of a big American car, loaded them into the VW, and ended up with room to spare while a voice advised, "When a big car isn't big enough, get a small car instead." A person could store a couple bodies or a few suitcases inside the Squareback's front trunk and still catch a roadside nap in back. It was a pack mule with style, and it set my expectations for vehicles unreasonably high.

My parents spent most of '77 and '78 helping Betty (my mother's mother) and her new husband, Don, build an A-frame on a ten-acre parcel of overgrown woods in Brown County—a location that shares my middle name. Matthew and I internalized early on that we should call Betty *Grandma* to her face and use her first name in the presence of our parents and their siblings. Betty had once driven her Buick through the front of a Kentucky Fried Chicken. In the newspaper article about the ordeal, it was noted, "No one was injured, but the driver had to be sedated at the scene." Even more impressive, she had married Don Chaney, who, someone had told us, was the grandson of Lon Chaney, a groundbreaking silent-film actor known as "the man with a thousand faces." He'd played the Phantom of the Opera and the Hunchback of Notre Dame. This made us third-degree relations to fame, by marriage.

The drive to our grandmother's land, resting halfway between Columbus (where we lived) and Bloomington (where Dad took classes), took thirty minutes each way. In a state flatter than any other, aside from West Texas, perhaps, Brown County is a pocket of creeks, thickets, and rolling hills the glaciers missed—a Hoosier's Vermont.

Though I knew my brother played with me on those rides to make the best of his confinement, this understanding did not diminish my delight in our long games of I spy and slugbug. All four of us attempted to hold our breath between the two signs marking the entrance and exit of a tiny town called Gnaw Bone. These rides were my happy place: the droning motor, whirring wheels, and the smell of sun-warmed upholstery as positively charged as Christmas trees and birthday cake.

After Gnaw Bone came Little Nashville. There we'd turn right, pass the Little Opry and the quaint wooden storefronts erected to attract tourists, then drive another five miles into the hills to find Betty's place. Matthew and I spent those Brown County days swinging from tree vines, sailing over the water of Betty and Don's manmade lake. We poked Moby Dick, the gigantic imported catfish, with a stick and watched his ghostly white antenna search through the murk of the water for the source of his injury. We dug holes big enough to hide pint-size soldiers in battle, the dirt under our nails making its way into our mouths, so that every month or so we got pinworms. Back home each Sunday, our mother felt behind our ears and through our hair, using the head of an extinguished match and her long fingernails to loosen the ticks from our skin.

Near the end of the Brown County project, I nestled my body between the studs of two walls while waiting inside the A-frame for the adults to say their goodbyes. It was summer, so I wore only a terrycloth romper. The soft pink stuff that lined the wall behind me reminded me of cotton candy, and I leaned in to it, wiggling back and forth. My mother noticed first and let out an *Oh no.* The stinging set in before she ran over and pulled me out — my arms, legs, and neck on fire with tiny slivers of fiberglass. Mortified and in pain, I ran to the car for comfort and curled into the fetal position in the rear cargo area.

From the time I was youngest, I was known as the most volatile member of my extended family tree, traveling down the branches of both my maternal and paternal sides. While my tantrums always had a trigger, such as the insulation or a knotted shoelace, those around me seemed to never understand the reasons for my upset. My earliest memories are flashes of screams and tears and my mother rolling her eyes, saying, *There goes Missy again.* By the time I was two, Mom was the only person who felt comfortable being alone with me. Even my father avoided taking me on a solo trip to the convenience store for fear something might trigger an explosion. I had big feelings, and they drove away those I loved.

It was Matthew who followed me to the Squareback that day —

a small but real act of kindness. He hid in the backseat and put on a puppet show for me with his constant companion, Animal from *The Muppet Show*. Animal told joke after joke, which I appreciated. There was little worse in one of my rages than being ignored, though I didn't stop crying until we started driving.

The buzzing of the engine and the sway of the road calmed me so entirely that I was half asleep by the time our favorite song came on the radio. The song, we thought, was written for us because it has a line about Lon Chaney Jr., son of Lon Chaney, who in our imaginations was a relative of sorts.

I saw Lon Chaney Jr. walkin' with the queen, doin' the werewolves of London.

Dad knew how much we loved the song, so he turned it up. I climbed from the cargo area into the backseat with Matthew, and we danced as best we could in that low-roofed space, the drive wheels humming beneath us, my parents laughing as I moved my arms through the air like a disco ballerina and Matthew karate-chopped invisible bad guys in time to the beat.

"Hold my hand!" Matthew yelled over the music.

I wanted little more than to grab on to his outstretched hand, but most everything with him ended up being a joke on me.

"Come on, Missy," he begged in that voice I could not refuse.

I grabbed hold and he swung our arms back and forth like we were doing a dance on *The Gong Show*. Our dad sang along while Mom clapped, and when the song ended, Dad called us a couple of little shavers. "Again!" we chanted, singing our own version of the song.

Aaahoo! Werewolves in the night . . . Aaahoo! Werewolves in the night . . .

Dad pulled into the fast lane, deepening my delight.

"Again," I said to Matthew.

He looked at me with my same eyes and held out his hands on a drive and a day so perfect, I forgot to hurt.

Again. Again. Again — the whole way home.

When we weren't on the road, Matthew treated me like a stranger. With our dad engaged in a Bob Vila–style remodeling project and Mom working nonstop at her homemaking tasks, we were free to roam our neighborhood. Matthew had a habit of pulling into his orbit the kind of people others might go out of their way to avoid. He adored all the World Wrestling Federation characters, our local garbage men, carnival workers, daredevils of any kind, and a boy my age named Gary Wayne who had Down syndrome and a Big Wheel. He was most impressed by the black man across the street (rumored to be an ex-con) who answered the door shirtless one Halloween and said, "Candy? Kid, I ain't got no fucking candy."

We lived near one of two graveyards in Columbus. I spent whole days tracking my brother there, riding silent as a spy on my very first bike: a white Schwinn cruiser with red streamers and a blue banana seat. Matthew ran with a pack of friends while I followed them — uninvited. I don't recall having many friends of my own, and to this day I can't tell you why, except that I was then how I have always been: driven, quiet, moody, and a few degrees withdrawn.

The summer I was five, my father's parents, Benny and Eunice, passed through one afternoon on their annual trip to Florida. Dad was at work and Mom out running errands for a short hour while Matthew and I stayed home alone, watching cartoons. My mother loathed how her in-laws, who lived over an hour away, dropped by unannounced every few months. It was an action too country for her, uncivilized. *Why can't they call ahead like everyone else?* she'd say. Dad would answer with a smile and a shrug. I was glad she wasn't home to get upset about it when my grandparents showed up at the door that morning.

Both survivors of the Great Depression, Eunice and Benny made most everything—food, children, lye soap, quilts, a farm. Benny was a man of fewer words than my father, even. He was a World War II veteran who supposedly guarded the *Enola Gay* for five whole minutes just days before the Hiroshima bombing. Approval and praise were not part of their family vocabulary. Mamaw was never mean, but instead all business with occasional bouts of laughter. Her demeanor fascinated and frightened me. Matthew and I spent a week or two each summer at their farm, sleeping in the same bed that my father had shared with his brothers back in the day. Because of Matthew's missing front teeth, Mamaw used to cut the corn we picked off the cob for him so he could eat it. He loved that small kindness from an otherwise hard woman.

The curse of being born ambitious is that I loved most those who showed few signs of loving me back. My brother claimed the top rung of my heart, his general dislike of me so obvious. My dad's regular absences brought him in second, and my Mamaw came in third. My mother loved me through and through. She showed it every day, with her attention to the color of ribbon in my hair, the chapter books she read to us each night, and the way she'd drop a Stephen King novel without even marking the page to check on me if I so much as coughed. Though I knew I would crumble without her, that my sense of adventure was built on the foundation of her unconditional love, I took her for granted. Her heart was a contest won, an award achieved.

On the summer day when my grandparents passed through Columbus on their way to Florida, I didn't think about my mother at all as I begged my way into the backseat of their new Chrysler—a prize my father was stunned to discover they could afford, considering he'd been raised on so much homegrown corn that to this day it is a food he will not touch. It turned out my grandparents weren't poor so much as they were tight with money. From retirement onward, they lived slim but well. I packed my tapestry suitcase and used every tool of manipulation in my skill set to persuade them to take me. Matthew returned to his cartoons, uninterested.

I watched from the rear window of the New Yorker as Papaw pulled away from our house and we wove through town, past our Presbyterian church, and Columbus's copper-roofed courthouse, and onto the interstate. From there, south toward the Ohio River and the green hills of Kentucky beyond it.

Did Matthew watch from the window as we left, or was he too deep in *Looney Tunes* to notice? Did he feel abandoned, or anxious for our mother to come home and discover his only competition for her affections vanished? Either it never occurred to me to consider my brother's feelings beyond his growing animosity toward me, or I didn't yet have the capacity to see beyond my own wants and needs.

No more than a dozen miles into our drive to Florida, I both wanted and needed air conditioning. The burgundy velour of the New Yorker's seats turned damp under my sweating legs. All the windows were rolled up, and the black vehicle was a magnet for the sun. It took me almost an hour of sweating to work up the will to make a request.

"Could we open the windows?"

"Vents are open," Mamaw said.

"But I'm hot."

"Windows are fire exits," she told me.

Fire exits? In hindsight, I realize the turbulence likely messed up her hair, which she set overnight once a week so that brown curls engulfed her head like a helmet. Too stunned for a comeback,

I sweated for two days straight in that luxury sedan. My cheeks pulsed red, but I would not complain. After all, we were going places.

We stopped at a flea market where Mamaw bought me a cardboard box filled with everything I needed to weave potholders. By the time we arrived in Florida, I'd made a dozen, and Mamaw had sewn the face of a full-size quilt out of squares salvaged from used clothing.

For two weeks in Florida, I wore my rainbow-stripe bikini and red sunglasses, the ocean rolling up to my toes as tiny white crabs chased the tide. I got saltwater up my nose and collected spider crabs in a bucket. Papaw caught something called a grunt fish that made noises like a tiny pig when he pulled it from the water, and a ten-year-old boy down the beach from us got sideswiped by a hammerhead shark.

I don't recall thinking much about my family the whole time I was gone, and the ruckus my departure caused went over my head. Our mother had returned from grocery shopping to find her kindergartner transported across state lines for two weeks without parental consent. I didn't mean to hurt anyone. Wanderlust is a trait I was born with, as innate to me as charisma was to Matthew. I came home happy and tan and ready to do it all over again. The world now felt so irrevocably wide and wild to me that I could hardly believe it had existed all along, and I knew then that I would leave home forever the first chance I got.

Not long after my return, the Mustang started making a strange noise when we crossed the railroad tracks (a daily occurrence in our town). The tires, Dad noticed, were wearing in an uneven pattern. My mother took it in for an alignment one day while Matthew and I played at the neighbor's house. When she came back, her face looked like a deflated balloon. She'd walked the two miles from the shop and went to lie down, leaving us to guess at the bad news.

That night, as she and my father talked in the kitchen, we heard her recount her final moment with the Mustang: *I watched as they put it up on the lift. A front wheel came clean off when it left the ground. He said the axle had broken and only the weight of the car was keeping the wheel on.*

My father seemed more impressed than frightened. When it came to the Mustang, he always saw a glass half full. This was a story not of how the car had almost killed us (though that's the way my mother saw it). It was a story of how the Mustang had protected us by hanging on to that single wheel with every pound she had.

I heard a pause, in which I imagine my mother insisted Dad meet her gaze. *I drive the kids all over town in broken-down cars. I'm tired of it. It's not safe.*

Instead of investing in the Mustang, my parents sold it to the mechanic for a hundred bucks. It's a story that made such an impression on me that I have to remind myself I was never there, though I can still see the look on the mechanic's face when he put her on the lift and watched the rear wheel fall off. I know the quality of light that came through the panes of glass on garage door, and the sound the tire made when it hit the ground. I kept the story alive by writing each word down in my head.

I don't remember saying goodbye to the Mustang or the Squarebacks. They were simply here one day and gone the next.

My father made my mother a single promise to soothe Mom's angst. He agreed to visit a place my family had never been: the new car lot. A new car was a luxury beyond what I dreamed possible at that age, the kind of luxury my own kids would not know until they were five and eight — each a year north of the ages Matthew and I were when we rode home in the back of a 1978 sky-blue Volaré.

August 6, 2000

What else happened to Matthew that final Sunday? Here are a few things I know, from the wreckage he left behind:

The answering machine blinks red. Had she called? Was it her? The dog rubs against his master's legs, cat-like, trying to scratch his flea-bitten back. His was the most effeminate junkyard dog imaginable — a detail that always gave Matthew a kick. She had loved the dog too. So she said.

Good dog, Early Times. You big fairy.

He stares at the machine on his dresser, wanting to hear every word but afraid of what the sound of her voice might do to him. He lights a smoke, hits play.

It is her. She is crying, tired, or both, and says miss you *and* fuck you *and* divorce *and* I love you.

He thinks for a moment about what time it is in L.A. but stops himself. He will not call back. He's not sure which is harder: staying away from booze or staying away from her. Both became unbearable this week, like being nailed into a crawlspace and left for dead with spiders and rats. He figured he'd rather take his chances with booze because he knows, has known: She's the death of him. His wife.

I love you.

So she says.

THREE

Plymouth Volaré

Indiana: 1970s–1991

I DON'T KNOW A THING ABOUT money, but the way my mother puts on her red lipstick and matching heels tells me we're bluffing. There are rows of cars, lined up by color and model, and I want to take one home before someone asks us to leave. Soon I'm standing eye-to-window with a blue sedan. Dad speaks to the salesman in a voice too low for me to hear over the wind. He shifts his weight from one foot to the other, his brow tight enough to hold a dollar in the crease. When the salesman unlocks the door, I settle myself in to the rear bench seat and fold down the armrest. The door closes behind and I sit there, alone in this car they call a Volaré. The hum of the wind stills me as my family carries on outside like actors on a movie screen. The new-car smell invades my sinuses and opens my head. Blue vinyl doors, matching carpet, and tapestry on the seats.

Soon Dad climbs in the driver's seat, my mother in the passenger seat, my brother beside me — smiling, even — as the engine revs. We pull off that lot and on to the streets of Columbus before anyone tells us not to. We weave through town to the country and back again, my parents' laughter broken only by rounds of a song they belt out in broken voices: *Volaré! Volaré!*

It is ours and brand new, and I would sleep, eat, and live inside until I could drive my way out if they'd let me. Because this is how you do it. This is all you need. A car is a ticket, a ticket is a bootstrap, and when you find a bootstrap you grab on and pull.

Inspired by the oil crisis of '73, Plymouth introduced a new "economy" sedan halfway through '76. With a boxy body and a rear and front nearly equal in length, this new product replaced the larger Dodge Dart, Plymouth Valiant, and Plymouth Duster. The Volaré promised a "big-car ride" in what was to the American automaker at the time a compact frame. But calling the Volaré a small vehicle is a bit like calling a cougar a cat. With a slant-six engine revered for longevity and reliability and a special axle system created to absorb the impact of the road, the Volaré offered the boat-ride feel consumers wanted at a price that made a new car attainable for a working-class family like ours. Plymouth plugged the Volaré as "a new kind of American small car" that would save owners "trips to the gas station." The pitch worked on my parents.

In the end Plymouth considered the Volaré a flop, but it remains (for me) the model that came closest to the Platonic ideal of *car* ever made. Our baby-blue sedan looked like the car a child might draw given no direction (imagine the family car on *The Simpsons* — right angles from bumper to bumper).

Of course I didn't know any of this or think this way then. All I knew was that the Volaré and I bonded hard on sight. She set my template for *car* as much as my dad was *man* and my mother *woman.* Part accomplice, part heroine, she was our ride from the time I had baby teeth to the time my first menstrual pad lurked like a damp, dark secret below me. She was our Mystery Machine, our General Lee, our Herbie, our K.I.T.T., though we only ever called her by her factory-made name, Volaré. That slant-six engine steady as our parents' love. Mom often caught me cribbing my teeth on the vinyl that lined the top of the Volaré's fat door. I'd already gotten in trouble for devouring the edge of our walnut coffee table, the feel of damp, splintering wood soothing me as I watched Saturday-morning cartoons. Yet I loved the car door best, the material warm and slippery, my teeth marks visible but impermanent. Mom would shake her head and swat at me from the front seat, saying, *You're going to break the door or your teeth, Miss.*

In the Volaré, we played *Dukes of Hazzard* all over the Sears parking lot — our father doing donuts, burning rubber, and sending us sailing over speed bumps so fast that a time or two my head grazed the ceiling, our mother saying *Stop it, Keith, come on now, stop it* the whole while.

Our mother used the Volaré as her karaoke machine, solo performing the Meat Loaf duet "Paradise by the Dashboard Light" more times than I can recall. She sang both parts as we feigned embarrassment. She hand-danced like a Motown singer, pausing to croon certain lines to my father as he drove. Though she couldn't goad Dad into joining her, he smiled through the entire eight-minute routine, down to the fadeout on the final words: *It was long ago and it was far away and it was so much better than it is today* . . .

There was that time Mom drove us to the store that used to be Airway but then became Target and I held a few damp bills in my hand, hoping to buy my first vinyl. Matthew had already seen Kiss in concert (twice). I asked him to help me find that "dancing" song I kept hearing on the radio. I sang a couple bars: *Come dancing* . . . Matthew smiled and pressed David Bowie's *Let's Dance* into my arms. The cover wasn't what I'd expected, but he assured me that was what I wanted. I bought it, took it home, and was heartbro-

ken to find I'd wasted my only cash on the wrong dancing song. I
let Matthew borrow it. The dark and sultry sounds of that album
rose up through the heating vent that connected us as I lay in bed,
listening, the music working its way into me like foxtail grass in a
dog's ear.

One time, as Mom drove a carload of kids across town, a rear
door swung open while she took a curve at thirty. I'd stayed un-
buckled to accommodate the four kids in the backseat with me,
and the force of the curve pulled my torso and arms out the door.
Matthew, sitting so close beside me that our legs still touched,
watched my fall with amazement, doing nothing to reel me in. The
friend next to him grabbed my shirt and yanked me back inside.
Afterward, my mother pulled over to recover from the near tragedy. Matthew's friend punched his arm and broke the stunned silence with the words *What the hell, Stephenson?*

I don't know if it was then that I first realized my brother's feelings for me were complicated at best, or if it was the time he told
me to stand in front of a fat oak tree while he threw Chinese stars
at my head. (For years telling this story I added the detail that he'd
tied me to the tree, but that's not true. All he had to do was tell me
to stand there, and I did. His will was the only tether I needed.)
Or maybe it was the time I was seven and talked my way onto his
BMX bike team. On a drive back from a dirt track in Indianapolis,
the thirty-something team owner, Andy, gave Matthew a Schwinn
T-shirt — in trade for Matthew making me hold Andy's sweaty
right hand while he steered with his left. Or maybe it was the time
I stole and replaced an ACDC tape of Matthew's and he retaliated
by slipping a drawing of me under my door, arrows piercing my
body parts, connecting to words like *leg stubble, Bermuda shorts,
feet big as boats.* That drawing is the image I still see when I think
of twelve-year-old me.

Eventually not even my parents would argue that my brother loved me, which is why his love became my deepest ambition, the thing I was most driven to get. But we continued to fall apart before we came together. The rear seat of the Volaré is the only place I remember us in proximity during these years.

Once I entered elementary school, I channeled the big feelings that had fueled my epic tantrums into pure, unrefined ambition. My mother, who had given up dreams of being a real, live runway model in order to have kids, led the way. She enrolled me in figure skating and ballet lessons at the age of four, lessons I would continue through middle school. I auditioned for every community theater production and landed roles in the chorus. I was an "Indian" in *Peter Pan* and spent hours doing homework backstage, all my school papers smudged with "Red Texas Dirt" makeup that we powdered over our pale skin with a giant puff. I joined the church choir and my school choir. When I got old enough, I became a cheerleader. I recall stints on the swim team and diving team as well. The flute I picked up in middle school.

I was more a creepy, jealous kind of ambitious than a healthy kind. To this day, I recall the words and hand motions of my best friend's solo from our second grade Christmas pageant. Wendy Williamson and I were inseparable, but I doubt I even pretended to be happy for her when she got cast in the lead role that year — Father Time. She was prettier than me, and nicer. At home, in my bedroom mirror, I practiced Wendy's Father Time solo again and again so that I might be prepared to save the day in case something terrible happened to her just before curtain.

In my downtime, I read books and built my own cassette collection: show tunes, the Boss, Madonna, and Cyndi Lauper (music Matthew more or less loathed). I specialized in bizarre routines, like putting on my faux Ray-Bans and white choir gloves and rigging a strap to my keyboard so I could pretend to play while lip-synching Billy Joel's "Piano Man." Mom would make the whole family sit and watch these routines, which only deepened the divide between Matthew and me.

I didn't do all this because I was talented and beautiful. I was too serious and bossy to be charming, but I was a petite tornado of sorts. I'm a slim person of average height to this day, my weight my entire adult life just breaking triple digits. In elementary school, I was a bona fide beanpole. My knees were the fattest part of my legs, my neck conspicuously long, my head small, my nose and feet oversize. My mother encouraged me in everything artistic, but even she could see I was not the sunny beauty-pageant princess she had hoped for. Still, she shuttled me from one activity to another in the Volaré, our dinners bought from drive-throughs and devoured from Styrofoam containers in the car. I can tell you for a fact that there was no gravy on earth that could mar the Volaré's sky-blue upholstery.

The Volaré was there for me when I broke my leg cheerleading in sixth grade and had to cancel my trip to Space Camp. It was the final game of the season — a special parent/student game with no uniform required. I wore electric-blue eye makeup, curled my bangs into a righteous bear claw, and sported my favorite jeans with zippered ankles. My mom joined in for the halftime cheer. I was the smallest, the loudest, the most serious of all the cheerleaders, my robotic moves executed with the force and precision of a soldier. At the end of the routine, I jumped onto my mother's back — a simple mount — and then jumped off. My left ankle rolled. I felt the snap, then a sensation like sodapop running up my leg. Broken. A spiral fracture traveling four inches up my tibia. I remained on the court, alone in front of packed bleachers, until my mom realized what had happened and some random father carried me to the Volaré.

It was night and I was terribly thirsty, so I asked my mom if she would swing by a drive-through for a soda. I leaned against a rear door, my legs stretched across the bench seat. Mom assured me I could have a soda at the hospital. As she gunned the engine on the fifteen-minute drive there, my lower left leg swelled up so that my jeans fit tight as a sausage casing. Each time we hit a bump or took a turn, my left foot hinged from the shin, my knee arrow straight. I ended up on the couch for a week in a cast that stretched from hip to toe, and a walking cast after. When my left leg saw the full light of day again two months later, it took me weeks to get my old walk back. I can still feel bumps from the calcium deposits that bound my shinbone back together as I healed.

While I turned into an Alex P. Keaton of the performing arts world, Matthew was a reluctant Fonzie in our household, coming up from his basement lair at random times, entertaining us with a joke or story, and wandering off to find his tribe. I had activities, and Matthew had friends. Others gravitated to him and engaged in his strange plans, such as going to the Salvation Army to buy polyester bell-bottoms and white pleather loafers, because, why not? I looked like I had just wandered out of an Olan Mills portrait as much as they looked like lost members of the Beastie Boys. No matter how hard I tried, I could never navigate that kind of cool. Some gifts we are born with. Matthew took the motherlode in magnetism.

By the time Matthew started middle school, the Volaré wasn't so young anymore. Most of our friends' parents drove small, compact sedans — Hondas or Toyotas. The Volaré stood out like a blue beast in the parking lot. Matthew grew so ashamed of her that he insisted Mom let him out two blocks from his middle school, the same school where she'd taken a job as the librarian's aide. I'd ride the rest of the way with Mom to catch my school bus, which ran from the middle school to the country school. I had to ride an hour each way to attend the nearest gifted and talented program. The ride I saw as a bonus. While I waited for that flat-faced Bluebird to depart, I'd watch my brother swagger by, his head shaved with the family dog clippers, his Converse duct-taped together. He was as bright as ever when he wanted to be, but something inside him had gone dormant, underground, like a cicada.

During his freshman year of high school, Matthew ran away after his first ever bigtime girlfriend tried to break things off. She loved him, but it was spring and she was a senior and thought it kinder to end things instead of letting them drag on. Jennifer Jones carried the same name as one of our mother's favorite silver screen stars, a detail that elevated her elegance and beauty in my eyes.

My family fell into a slow but growing panic over my brother's absence. It was the first time I'd seen our parents truly worried. Mom and her siblings more or less raised each other after their father's death, and our dad grew up in a pick-your-own-switch kind of family. As a reaction to their own upbringings, our folks tried to be our friends more than they tried to parent us. It was an admirable attempt to turn what they'd learned in the late sixties into a parenting philosophy. We would all be individuals with equal say. We would be groovy. No one would be a drag. From their perspective, things had turned out pretty well. While their teenage years had been filled with accidents, death, and pregnancy, Matthew and I grew up in *Leave It to Beaver* Land in comparison. Our parents loved us unconditionally and enjoyed our stories, pastimes, and shenanigans as much as we enjoyed entertaining them, which was a lot.

During the runaway episode, all of Mom's siblings drove down from Lebanon, and our house because a headquarters of sorts, the coffeepot full at all hours, the fridge stocked with Coors and Chardonnay. In an attempt to find Matthew, our aunt Beth bought a miniskirt and some Reebok high-tops and went undercover amongst the street kids of Bloomington. She was our youngest aunt, married to my mother's only brother. She took with her a picture of Matthew holding her daughter Katie, our cousin. In the photo, Katie is three, with blond curls, smiling up from my brother's lap. Aunt Beth showed that image to a kid in an arcade who looked like he could be one of Matthew's friends, and said, "Do you know this boy? Because this little girl is my daughter, and she needs him to come home." In trade for a gas station sandwich, the kid led Aunt Beth to a condemned Victorian house where she found Matthew on a mattress in the basement, sick and lost. She drove him to the nearest Burger King, where he ate two Whoppers, fries, and a shake before the color returned to his face. They waited there for my parents to arrive in the Volaré while I sat at home with Jennifer Jones, envious of the way she cried out of only one eye.

In the months that followed, Mom and Dad kept a tighter eye on Matthew, which he resented. He'd mumble things at dinner about how he knew they were planning to pay some hippies a bunch of money to abandon him in the woods for two weeks with a canteen and a sleeve of Saltine crackers. His new German girlfriend, Natalie—a pink-haired member of a military family—had told him these horror stories about her own Outward Bound experience. I was miffed to learn this Outward Bound camp served only "problem" kids. I'd have traded my middle-of-nowhere town for a real wilderness faster than I'd once packed a suitcase for Florida. Our folks assured Matthew they weren't sending either of us anywhere, but he kept pushing. He let the Bs and As he earned with little effort drop to Cs and Ds.

The middle school where Mom worked sat across the street from the high school. Students from both schools were allowed to walk a block away to the Taco Bell, Dairy Queen, and the local deli for what they called "off-campus lunch." Matthew joined the punks who smoked cigarettes on a corner near the high school tennis courts during the lunch hour.

"I saw you on Cancer Corner," Mom said to him one day after school, the tone in her voice snapping me out of my *Brady Bunch* trance.

Matthew stared back. "Yeah?"

"Yeah. I don't like it."

He stood before us in his black leather jacket and put on the meanest smile I'd ever seen him give our mother. It spread across his face like a disease. "Don't worry, Mammy. I ain't gonna steal your Vagina Slimes."

Mom stared back, her mouth hanging open like she'd just been whacked with a hard object.

He blew right by her and out the back door.

Our mother was a closet smoker of Virginia Slims, and by closet I mean she didn't like for us to mention her habit and only smoked inside our house, in front of every friend and family member we knew. For Matthew to use his crude nickname for her smokes, along with intentionally bad grammar, all while addressing her as Mammy? It was jab wrapped in an insult topped with misogyny and racism. His between-the-words message to her something like *You think you can shame me? You can't think anything bad about me I haven't thought first.*

I responded to shame by crying in dark spaces. He responded by mimicking the broken image he felt others projected onto him. He'd smile, get snide, go low. I'm not sure if you'd call that passive-aggressive or flat-out aggressive. Either way, it was punk rock. It was hostile.

A kid with a chip on his shoulder, looks to rival James Dean's, and a sense that he has nothing to lose is a hard son to parent. The era of being friends exploded in our folks' faces, and I didn't help.

· · ·

At the dinner table on a rare evening when my father came home from work on time to join us, he praised Matthew for pulling a D up to a C, which was probably an oversight on my brother's part. He could ace tests without studying, so failure took a real effort. My father went on about how good it was to see the old grades coming up. Our mother nodded emphatically, reinforcing Dad's words with her listener noises. Matthew stared at them like they were stupid, and my face turned pink over my plate of microwaved peas and chicken. I earned all As, all the time. I worked hard for them, and when I hit a mental roadblock, I collapsed into hot tears, so disgusted with myself that I couldn't lip-synch a single song until I'd mastered fractions or the art of the book report.

Our parents marveled at how they brought such different children into the world, and Dad (who does not believe in coincidence) would later suggest that our differences were cosmically ordained for our spiritual growth. Whether our natures were so disparate by luck or by design, there is no doubt that Matthew was my perfect foil: He did whatever he wanted and everyone loved him while I ran my tires bare trying to do everything "right," a single-mindedness that put a serious dent in my likability.

That night, after dinner, I couldn't let my brother's C go. I put on my pointe shoes and stalked my father as he snacked on chips and watched college basketball in the breakfast nook. I tried to engage him by talking about my straight As, fishing for praise in still waters as my feet cycled through a nervous series of relevés and ronds de jambe. When I couldn't get him to take his eyes off the screen for fear of missing one of Steve Alfred's famous three-pointers, or Bobby Knight throwing a folding chair, I spouted out this: "What if I start getting Fs? I could do it, you know. I could just fail."

Dad looked at me, irritated, but I wouldn't stop.

"Sometimes I feel like Matthew could take a dump on a paper

plate and you'd all just laugh, but I could become the first female president and you wouldn't even care."

Dad sighed, catching my drift. "You're two different kids, Miss. You have different strengths, different challenges."

The way he shrugged off my concern enraged me. "You," I said, "you don't know anything about discipline."

Dad slapped a hand down hard on the table. "I don't know anything about discipline?"

He shot me a look of disgust I'd not seen from him before, and haven't since. Then he got up and walked away.

That line I'd been probing? I'd found its electric boundary. Our father was a gentle mystic who loved fast cars, Tom Waits, home improvements, Carl Jung, and Jesus. But he was still our patriarch — a role that he honored by mortgaging his happiness for our own. His compulsive work ethic kept the fridge stocked, the cars running, and our house comfy. Dad had grown up in a home where discipline meant physical correction. Discipline had not made him happy, and he would not inflict such rigid paradigms on his children. He seemed to know already that I would turn out more or less fine in the same way he intuited that slapping rules and boundaries on his son would only strain their connection. For me to question our father like that, when he had sacrificed to provide me with a level of privilege unknown to him as a child, was a disgrace.

Oddly satisfied, I went back to performing my role as full-time pursuer of perfection, shuttled to every practice in the Volaré: my chariot, white knight, Old Faithful, harborer of ballet shoes, leotards, sheet music, Judy Blume books, figure skates, and my larger-than-life daydreams of finding a way beyond state lines for good.

August 6, 2000

He doesn't want to be here. Why is he still here? Who and what for? He drinks water from the faucet, opens a can of pork and beans, takes a cold spoonful, and gags it back up. The only way now is to keep drinking. Hair of the dog turned into ounces, liters, now gallons. He pours the beans into the dog's bowl. The dog. What about his dog?

He grabs a vodka bottle from the freezer and presses it against the goose egg on his head, remembering falling off the bench but not how he got home. The truck shines in the sun, paint off-the-lot good, right where he parked it three days ago. At least he didn't drive.

He finds a box of strawberry Jell-O and starts mixing up a batch of shots. Sunday. He finds that last mix tape his sister sent him and plays the Velvet Underground song she says she listens to on Sundays. He could call her, but where does she live now? Texas yet, or Montana still?

His folks. He should call, but what would he say?

Instead, he sits down and listens. Sunday morning... and I'm falling... I've got a feeling... I don't want to know.

FOUR

The Hondas

Indiana and Michigan: 1988–91

*N*EAR THE END OF THE EIGHTIES, Mom tired of the Volaré and bought herself a brand-new Honda Civic. She got a deal by snatching up an '88 still left on the lot at the start of '89.

"I talked him down to invoice price," she told everyone who commented on her new car. "Then I asked him to throw in the floor mats."

My mother knew how to drive a bargain, and I pitied the repairman or salesperson who tried to pull one over on her.

At some point just before or after she bought the Civic, our father scouted a used Honda CRX for himself. It was an ideal ride for him because it rode low like a racecar and had a zippy engine, but it was also a hatchback that got good gas mileage.

In one short decade, we'd bootstrapped our way over the poverty line and into a facsimile of a middle-class lifestyle. Dad's graduate degree in social work hung on the wall of the house we'd moved to partway through the eighties. It was one of those bungalows that arrived by train in the 1930s, each board part of a kit sold by Sears and Roebuck. In the sixties the owners added a two-car garage and an in-ground swimming pool. It was smaller than our white two-story house near the cemetery, but it sat on the better side of the park, directly across from the tennis courts. Our mother demanded we buy it, and in no time dad remodeled the basement, adding a bar, living area, third bedroom, second bath, and his office. Dad worked as a therapist at a respected private practice. People assumed he was a partner when in fact he was a contract employee. The same people also mistook our mother for the real middle school librarian instead of an assistant with a GED — a fact we grew weary of correcting.

Mom had a knack for creating the illusion that we had one hundred dollars for every dollar we spent. She bought us both a small collection of name-brand clothing each fall so that we might have a taste of whatever Izod, Ocean Pacific, Keds, or Converse item was in fashion. She enrolled us in art classes and sports of our choosing, even if she had to pay with a credit card. We looked and talked the part when Dad's bosses — the private practice partners with PhDs — invited us to dine with their families at houses in the fanciest subdivisions.

By the time the Hondas came along, I could pass for a doctor's kid. In fact, Mom set up playdates for me with several doctor's kids. One of them, Chrissy, was the daughter of the doctor who'd delivered me at Bartholomew County Hospital. I recall her house had two full stories, more bedrooms than residents, and wall-to-wall white carpet.

When Mom drove the Honda home for us to see, I wrinkled up my nose as if overwhelmed by the smell of a dead thing. I didn't like the new-car scent of its insides, the various shades of beige and brown, the low clearance, or the short, stubby trunk.

I crossed my arms, shifted my weight to one hip, and said these words in the same tone Matthew used whenever he said to me, *Nice face.*

"Nice rice burner, Mom."

While I understood this was a backdoor insult to my mother, I didn't yet see it as a slur against a culture. I was fourteen and ignorant, infected with a growing irreverence of unknown origin.

Mom smiled and shook her head. She knew my game, and she wouldn't let it diminish her victory.

Maybe I used the Honda as catalyst for separation from the parents I loved so I could become my own person. Or maybe I hated it out of allegiance to the Volaré. Or maybe it was a kind of auto snobbery I'd been steeped in that caused me to balk at the triangular lines of the thing. And maybe no small part of it was this discomfort I've had my whole life with the new and nice. Until just two years ago, almost all of my furniture and cars came to me secondhand. My guess is it was all of these reasons and more — an instinctive attempt to hold on to the part of our childhood Matthew and I would grow up and remember best, the wild part we never called poor or rich, the part where Dad partied on the couch with his halfway house friends and we ran around mostly naked while Mom sang along to the Beatles and we sometimes didn't have even enough money for McDonald's but the world felt like a thing cracked wide open, just for us.

Whatever my reasons, Mom shrugged off my discontent and kept us on the road to our bright future, the Volaré docked indefinitely in the driveway, near the trash cans.

The winter the Honda entered our lives, I applied to boarding school in secret. During a sleepover at a friend's house, I'd discovered a glossy brochure for a fine arts school located in the woods of northern Michigan. I asked my friend about it and she said it was some place for artist kids. She said her mother kept pushing her to apply, but she had no interest. She let me take the brochure home, and I read every sentence, studied every photo.

Though the words *boarding school* were as foreign to my family as *yacht, pâté,* or *cufflinks,* I sent away for my application and started the process without mentioning it. I wasn't trying to be sneaky. Though we'd done an admirable job of passing for middle class, I knew my parents couldn't afford the tuition. Still, I had to trust my instincts to knock on that door.

At the time I was an eighth-grader at the middle school where my mother worked. One day, while my English teacher chatted with my mother in the library, he mentioned how happy he was to write a letter of recommendation for me. My mother asked him what on earth he was talking about.

"Boarding school," he said. "Melissa is applying to boarding school."

I imagine my mother feigned knowledge of this, but truly I have no idea how she reacted to hearing such large news from someone other than me.

That night, I showed my parents the brochure, reciting the contents from memory. They admired and encouraged my ambition, but they did not want to give false hope. To humor me, as my mother said, they would drive us five hundred miles north in the brand-new Honda for my Interlochen audition.

Our route took us through the center of Indiana and along the western border of Michigan. We grazed the shoreline of Lake Michigan every now and then. It was March of 1989, and we hadn't expected the record-breaking St. Patrick's Day blizzard that descended on us. Flakes fell fat and thick enough that Dad could no longer make out any tire tracks on the interstate. The Honda — a front-wheel drive with a scant few inches of clearance and stock tires — handled like a small sled in that snow. Dad pulled off, guessing at the boundaries of the exit ramp. We coasted to a halt in a motel parking lot in the tiny town of Howard City, Michigan.

We had planned to make it to Interlochen that night, where a room at the campus lodge waited for us. My audition was scheduled for first thing the next morning. Mom made some calls and found out that they'd let me audition late if we could get there the next day. We walked across the only street in town, to the only establishment open and serving food — a bar and family restaurant. The place fell silent when we entered, and a large group of stern-looking folks wearing leprechaun hats and various shades of green glanced back at us. It was St. Patrick's Day — a holiday that passed unnoticed in my family. The people sat silently as we ate, waiting, perhaps, for us to leave so their party could begin.

In the morning, I found my bottle of gas station orange juice frozen solid on the inside ledge of the windowsill. I went into the bathroom hoping to warm up in the shower only to discover that the showerhead hung waist high and sputtered cold water like a kinked hose. I calmed myself by organizing my audition materials: a flute, ballet shoes, my writing portfolio, and two monologues. I'd be auditioning for theater, but I came prepared for four different majors, hoping that if I threw all my talents their way, one might stick.

We arrived on campus hours late and rushed straight to the theater building. Inside, suffering temporary blindness, I yelled out my first monologue: a grandmotherly character talking on a telephone in Neil Simon's *Plaza Suite*. An anxiety-induced frenzy overcame me. I likely could have levitated if I'd focused all my energy in an upward direction. When my performance ended, one of the two teachers conducting the audition asked me to sing "Silent Night." I'd grown up singing in choir and theater productions — my voice a steady but unremarkable contribution to the ensemble —

but terror rendered me tone deaf. The teachers made me sing it three times, joining in on the last few verses to help me find my register, but I was too far gone. I wanted only for the audition to end, which it did. As abruptly as we entered that dark theater, my parents and I were spit back out into the snow-filled day, blinded again.

"How'd it go?" Mom asked.

"Terrible," I said. "Let's hit it."

Furious with myself for delivering a performance nowhere near my best, I declined the campus tour and landed back home that night, nose buried in a novel enthralling enough to help me forget my own name.

At the end of the month, a slim letter arrived — for me, from Interlochen. I opened it in private on a school day, before my parents came home, so that I could process my rejection alone. I read it over and over, trying to wrap my head around the words on the page.

It was a formal acceptance to the theater department, bolstered by a fat scholarship. I was shocked, really, to find myself wanted by place where I'd bombed so badly. Perhaps the admissions committee pitied me. Perhaps they were low on theater majors that year. The second part of the letter — the financial aid information — was my real golden ticket. One simple paragraph informed me that Cummins Engine Plant — a company headquartered in Columbus — offered an outstanding scholarship for any student from my hometown.

And that's how I escaped Indiana: with dollars generated by some of the most revered and reliable diesel engines ever made.

I was fourteen the fall I filled a suitcase bigger than my own body with blue and navy clothing (Interlochen's uniform colors) and moved into a girls' dormitory on a campus filled with instruments and pine trees. Matthew was a senior in high school by then. He was a dead ringer for Keanu Reeves in the movie *River's Edge,* sporting already his lifelong uniform: shaggy hair, a concert T-shirt, Levi's, Converse, and a black leather jacket. Our parents took off that September on their very first cruise, leaving me to fly from Indianapolis to Traverse City alone, and Matthew to mind himself, I guess.

I loved being turned loose in O'Hare, and boarding that final plane to Michigan with a handful of other kids my age — all bound for Interlochen — felt like a living dream. Destiny in action.

I took to campus life pretty easily. I was self-sufficient, worked hard in my classes, kept to myself, and managed to get in and out of the cafeteria for meals without too much social anxiety. Interlochen was a school filled with creative kids, roughly two thirds of us on some form of scholarship. About four hundred students from all over the world came to live between two small lakes in the middle of the woods. The uniform policy made style a nonissue. You could wear store-bought clothes in navy and light blue, or opt for the free uniform — cords or knickers paired with button-down shirts, all from the 1960s.

My friend Victoria taught me how to use a pencil to secure my hair in a wild knot on the top of my head. Her roommate, Kiku, hid a rice cooker in their closet. Kitchen gadgets like this weren't allowed, but good rice made the distance between school and Japan tolerable for Kiku. We teased her about her "contraband," but she knew we'd never give her up. My friend Ben from Boston played a violin that could pay off my parents' mortgage. My roommate Tami took ski vacations in Colorado and cried the first week when she cut into a care package with an X-Acto knife and slit the shell of her Patagonia jacket.

"What's Patagonia?" I asked. "Other than a place, I mean."

My friend Celeste was half French. Her other half, all Kennedy. As in, her mother was a branch on *the* Kennedy family tree.

Several kids from my school would go on to some level of fame. Juel Kilcher from Alaska ran off to Los Angeles and became Jewel. Little Sufjan from freshman-year PE class grew up to be the musical wonder Sufjan Stevens. My friend Josh rose to acting fame when he played a character by the same name in *The Blair Witch Project*. And one of the few theater majors who was kind to me — Bruno Campos — made a name for himself playing Christina Applegate's dashing neighbor Diego in a prime-time sitcom. Another theater major, Ryan Alosio, ended up on *Days of Our Lives* for a few years, a show I'd watched with my mother on and off in my youth.

But I didn't know any of this then. In the fall of 1989, we were all the most talented kids from our hometowns, thrown together in the Northwoods to vie for the same roles, for first-chair oboe, for visual art exhibitions, spots in the Jazz Ensemble, or the coveted role of Sugar Plum Fairy in our annual production of *The Nutcracker*.

Interlochen was better than the *Fame* movie I'd watched a dozen times. Only harder, because I was me and had no idea how to make friends in this land of big talent and colorful extroverts. The theater department, I soon discovered, was a hostile environment for a midwestern wallflower.

The first week of school, all theater majors had to audition for the acting company. This confused me, since I'd already auditioned to get into school. My second audition was equally terrifying, in front of the same two teachers I'd met in the spring. Neither smiled. After my monologue, Jude — the director of the program — fingered a large metal ring that hung on a black leather string on her neck and said, "You're a dancer."

I nodded and explained I'd taken ballet since I was four.

"Why aren't you a dance major, then?" she asked.

"My teacher says my feet on pointe look like a pair of dead fish." Which was true — I didn't have the arches for pointe work.

She wrote a quick note to David, the other teacher, who nodded in agreement. Then they dismissed me.

That evening, the acting company list was posted on the doors of all four dorms (two for boys, two for girls). Out of the thirty-some theater majors, every name was listed except for three freshmen — Ben Maddy, Jacqui Burda, and me. We would spend our first year as actors unable to audition for any kind of part. I got it. I was new. I would have to do what I did best — be patient and work hard.

I went to every class, read every book, kept my head down, and listened. Jude was loud and mean and scared everyone. The ring she wore around her neck was rumored to be a cock ring, not that I knew what that was, but it seemed dark and witchy — a sign that she was not to be messed with, or even looked in the eye.

I called home when I was feeling bad. I'd mope on the phone, unwilling to hang up and unable to offer more than monosyllabic answers. This habit drove my parents crazy. Mom got mad at me while Dad tried to reassure me. When I was having fun, I forgot about my folks.

Matthew I saw only when I flew home for Thanksgiving, Christmas, or spring break. He spent his time gone from our house for days already. My parents had shifted their goals to helping him make it through graduation. This truce kept things in our household peaceful but distant. No one told anyone else what to do.

In the spring of my freshman year, I took a course called Theater in Western Civilization that challenged me like no class I'd taken before. I was the only freshman allowed, and I loved it. We read *Antigone, Oedipus,* over half a dozen Shakespeare plays. I couldn't bring myself to speak in class, but I read every word of every assignment out of fear that the teacher would ask me a question and I'd be revealed a fraud — a country bumpkin let in on a corporate scholarship loophole. My classmates simply ignored me.

One day we all showed up to class and David, the teacher, wasn't there. After ten minutes, Ali, an outspoken student from Boston, and a few of his friends (all seniors) convinced everyone that classes had a ten-minute rule: If the teacher doesn't show after ten minutes, you can leave. I pretended to leave with them but felt weird about it, so I went to the bathroom and then back to class, where I read for a while, alone in the great, dark theater basement. David walked in and found me there. He was irate, demanding answers. Names. I explained what had happened with the ten-minute rule, and in the next class he called out Ali as the ringleader, pointing out to everyone that I was the sole student not in trouble.

First I'd been dismissed by my peers. Now they blatantly resented me.

I lost myself in Chekhov's Sonya, in Tennessee Williams's Laura.

And when Interlochen's only twenty-year-old senior took a fancy to me that spring, I stopped studying. I stopped trying so hard to be good. I found my first boyfriend and rode home in the backseat of the Honda after his graduation that spring, sullen and defiant, knowing I'd never see that Canadian percussionist again.

Afraid of going back to Indiana, I'd set myself up for the summer with an internship at a repertory theater company in Dobbs Ferry, New York, though first I'd spend a week at home. I returned just in time for Matthew's high school graduation, which was a big deal in our family. I sat among our relatives in the high school gym, the pack of us waiting for the *S* names to be called. If Matthew managed to cross the stage sober and receive that diploma, he would be the first grandchild on either side to graduate high school. When he appeared in his blue gown and black high-tops, his shoulder-length hair so like our father's in the seventies, we stood up and cheered until our palms stung and our voices cracked. Matthew shook hands with the principal, took the diploma, and walked off stage with that Paul Newman swagger he couldn't dial down if he tried.

Since I'd left home the previous year, Mom filled her empty nest with friends. Our house became an oasis where wine o'clock started the second Mom got home from school, around two, and lasted until she passed out near nine. It was as if she'd picked up where she'd left off at age seventeen — saving the party days she'd been denied then for mid-life. After all, our mother was only thirty-eight by the time we both left home. She made Matthew's graduation party an epic event filled with wine and beer and guests swimming in the pool out back.

Before everyone got too deep into drinking, our folks gave my brother an unexpected graduation gift. Dad tossed Matthew the key to our beloved Volaré. Matthew stared at them, stunned, as the key with the Chrysler emblem spun in the air and fell to his feet. He had no inclination toward ownership, no instinct for mobility. He laughed nervously at the key before picking it up and thanking Mom and Dad. After saying goodbye to our various relatives and drinking a token Coors Light, he took off on foot with his pack of friends. He was never without his entourage — a colorful group of Indiana renegades who seemed like a real-life video to every John Cougar Mellencamp song on the radio. I knew he was closer to these friends than he'd ever been to me.

I had no taste for alcohol, but I swam with my younger cousins for a bit and spent the rest of the evening packing my suitcase for New York. By the end of the week, I boarded a plane for LaGuardia, happy to be leaving home once more.

In New York I learned how to build my own wardrobe out of thrift shops finds, how to hang stage lights, sew costumes, make props,

and run lines with real actors. The interns were a group of teenagers living in dorms along with the cast and crew. We had no adult
supervision of any kind (a detail my parents didn't know). We took
Method classes with a classically trained actor who would show
up on the big screen years later as Jim Carrey's father in *The Tru-
man Show*. We took improv classes with a kind genius who would
go on to create the hit series *Sex and the City*. In his class, I mastered the art of saying yes to whatever an improv partner threw my
way — a skill that defined all of my choices that summer. I learned
how to empty half a carton of OJ and fill it back up with vodka. I
learned that smoking and drinking went together like peanut butter and jelly. I even learned how to transform a soda can into a pot-
smoking device. And I loved nothing more than visiting New York
City. I'd take the train in with a couple other interns. We'd shop
the thrift stores and wander down to St. Mark's Place and through
Union Square, in search of giant pizza slices and landmarks such
as CBGB. Sometimes I'd get on a subway train solo, slip a favorite
tape into my Walkman, and ride that train until it came full circle,
motion soothing me as it had in the Squarebacks or the Volaré a
decade before.

It was my mother who had first introduced me to New York City.
Growing up in Indiana, I could gauge a family's wealth by the vacations they took. If they went nowhere, like my dear friend Denise
who lived in a trailer park, they were poor. If they spent a week or
so at a relative's house each summer, within state lines, they were
a little poor, like us. (For years our idea of a vacation was a week on
Mamaw's farm without our parents and a week with our folks and
extended family at our great-grandparents' house in Russellville
during the county fair.) Families that drove to Florida for vacation
were middle class, and those that flew to Florida? Straight-up rich.
   My mother passed down to me her love of black-and-white mov-

ies and the glamour that adorned every frame. We studied the costumes of Rosemary Clooney and Vera Miles in *White Christmas*, discussing at length around our Christmas tree which costume we'd most like to have ourselves. We'd watch *Miracle on 34th Street* on repeat after we got our VCR. Mom would tell me over and over again how Natalie Wood was the most beautiful girl in the world, who grew up to be the most beautiful woman in the world, and how she drowned in her prime, in a manner equal parts suspicious and tragic. Mom would tear up a little, fancying herself Melanie from *Gone with the Wind*, when we both knew she was Scarlett at heart.

My mother would say repeatedly, every holiday season, *Can you imagine spending Christmas in New York City, Missy? Can you? Just imagine it. Imagine it.*

I imagined it. Often.

In early summer of my fifth grade year, my mother gave me the wildest, most unexpected gift of my life. She spied a travel deal in the newspaper: One day in New York City for ninety-nine dollars per person. She bought us two tickets. We flew out of Indianapolis in the wee hours one morning and hit the ground running. In a single day in New York City, Mom (who'd never before visited) took me to Bloomingdale's and bought me an Esprit sweater and a real pair of Guess jeans. She took me to Trump Tower, where we stared at water trickling down a giant wall in the lobby made of orange stone while Mom told me how much of that city Donald Trump owned. She walked us by the Empire State Building and the Chrysler Building, and through Central Park, where we paused at Strawberry Fields. She shed a few tears for John Lennon — the Beatle her sisters all understood was hers — and she mumbled something bad about Yoko before we walked on. She took me to a restaurant named Serendipity and bought me a drink called frozen hot chocolate, which was big as my head. As I drank it, she said, "Keep your eyes open. Barbra Streisand loves this place."

I'll recall my whole life the bone-deep ache in my legs after walking the streets of that towering city for eighteen hours. When we got back on the plane at midnight, Indiana bound, I was thinking I'd come back and live there one day. I thought I'd found it — the place where I should have been born, filled with people alive and going places. People like me.

While I was in New York with my theater tribe, Matthew made his first attempt to escape our native state. A few weeks after graduation, he filled the Volaré's backseat with a box of books and art supplies, a crate full of records, an army duffle, his black leather jacket, and the aquarium that held his big green iguana named Bud. He'd decided to move to Fort Collins, Colorado, because his best friend since kindergarten had moved there after graduation to attend a guitar-making program. He had no plan beyond crashing on his friend's couch while hunting for a job.

My father took an unprecedented week off work to help Matthew with the drive. It was the longest road trip my brother had ever taken. Garbage trucks, alleys, and dimly lit basements in the wrong part of town called to him, but not the road. Matthew drove, my dad said, maybe a few dozen of those twelve hundred miles. Dad took a plane back from Colorado and had barely settled in to work when Matthew called. He told Dad things were fine, that he didn't need help, but he was coming home. He never said why. He didn't have to. While we all saw him confident in his element, he withered outside of it.

Soon, at my parents' urging, he rented a room from one of his best friend's ex-wives and landed an assembly-line job at Arvin, a local factory that was known for producing the first tire pump back in 1919. He spent his summer working eight-hour shifts for a company similar to the one paying my way through art school, his paycheck built on the foundation of fixing someone else's wheels so they could drive. He hated it.

I didn't come back from my New York summer the same kid. What I mean, I guess, is that I didn't come back a kid at all. At Interlochen, the theater department didn't love me any more than it had when I was a freshman, despite my recent big-city experience working long hours in a repertory theater. Though I was finally allowed to audition for plays, I went the whole year (again) without being cast in a single role. I got depressed. I daydreamed about running away, back to New York City, like a kid from the previous year, Oliver Ray, who had Oxblood Docs that laced up to his knees. Rumor was he'd hitchhiked into Traverse City to catch a Greyhound to NYC, where he later became Patti Smith's young lover and collaborator. Who knew so much would change in a single year that I'd end up dreaming of running away from the place I'd run to?

I ate and slept and one night, with a friend, took a razor to my arm in that experimental, nonchalant way that was common in the girls' dorms. My friend cut often for reasons we didn't discuss. She made one cut, and said, *Your turn.* I made the smallest of chicken scratches and watched the cut bloom red. It felt so finite, tangible, a relief of sorts to point and say, *My wound is here.* But mostly it felt like nothing.

She cut again, and again nodded to me. My second wound split immediately down to the shimmery fat below the thin skin of my inner arm. I got worried and the next day went to health services with some wild story about how I injured my arm while cutting light gels for a play. The nurse gave me a Band-Aid and, by the time

I returned to my dorm, reported me to our house mother and the school counselor for self-injury.

Meetings were held. My parents were called. I ended up allowed to stay at school on the condition that I see a psychologist in Traverse City. My parents were worried, but I wouldn't — couldn't — talk to them. I had no words for this caught-between-worlds sickness I'd contracted. I wouldn't talk to the therapist either. He and I struck a deal — I'd take the Ritalin he prescribed me to combat my lethargy and daydreaming, and he'd let me go each session after a five-minute check-in, which gave me exactly fifty-five minutes to walk the grounds of the abandoned state psychiatric hospital and smoke cigarettes before the school van came to drive me back to campus. The Ritalin affected me in a fashion the opposite of what my therapist intended. I wasn't alert, I was catatonic. I slept through classes, sometimes up to twenty hours a day. I ate a lot and weighed more than I ever have since. I couldn't do much more than read poems, listen to songs, and take long walks through the snow to sneak cigarettes, which is how I passed that lonely Michigan winter — in a drug-induced hibernation.

By the time spring arrived, I was sixteen and had a new best friend — Celeste, the girl who was half French and half Kennedy. Celeste was a writing major, and she took me to hear the visiting artists read their work in the chapel on campus. I heard people like Rick Bass, Pam Houston, Gerald Stern, and Li-Young Lee in that sacred space. The experience flipped some circuit breaker buried in a far corner of my brain.

I ditched my Ritalin and started writing poems. I wrote about and around all the things that had happened to me, imitating the Sharon Olds and Sylvia Plath books I read until their spines cracked. Just before leaving for my second summer, I walked into the creative writing building with a pile of poems and knocked on the director's office door.

"Whaddya want?" he said. Delp was a white-haired, fly-fishing forty-something poet known to students by last name alone.

"I want to be a writing major."

He sized me up, straight-faced, then laughed. "That's a questionable endeavor. What are you now?"

"A theater major."

"That's the worst. I don't get theater. It's all fake. People just stand up there and pretend. You like that stuff? Who likes that stuff?"

I shrugged, not wanting to admit that I liked that stuff.

"Ha! See? All fake. Whaddya got there?"

I held out my poems and a change-of-major form.

Delp took the form and passed the poems back to me. "Look," he said. "I'm going to do you a favor. I'm not going to read those." He signed the form and handed it over. "Now take that to the office and I'll see you next fall. Got it, Stephenson?"

And I did. I got it. It is, to this day, one of the kindest acts of faith in my character anyone has ever committed. By believing in me, he made me better.

Still, I had a summer to kill before I could return to Interlochen a writer. Mom picked me up at the airport that May to take me to the house that now felt as awkward to me as a sofa draped in plastic, to the town where my brother lived but did not thrive, the town where I no longer had a single friend. It felt like a prison sentence. Mom drove that milquetoast Honda down I-65 faster than usual, anxious to make it home in time for happy hour.

Over drinks with her friends that afternoon, she delivered in my presence a line I would continue to hear my whole adult life: *The day Missy left for boarding school is the day I started taking Prozac.*

It is also the day she started washing her antidepressant down with bottomless glasses of white wine. I see now the wound she was tending. When she'd daydreamed about my NYC future, I'm sure she imagined herself there too, with weekends spent at my SoHo loft, and front-row tickets to every show opening. She assumed I'd take her with me.

I doubt she ever dreamed that by showing me a world beyond Indiana, she'd given me directions for abandoning her, the way her father had abandoned her when that semi took his life. The way her first boyfriend had abandoned her a year later when a car wreck crushed him. The way our father abandoned her daily, his eighty-hour workweeks rendering him half ghost in our house. And her son, whose heart moved on even before he moved out.

August 6, 2000

He downs three shots real fast before noon. What's the saying on that T-shirt his brother-in-law wears? If you want to drink all day, you gotta start in the morning.

The alcohol pinks his cheeks, and he laughs.

He loves everyone so much it hurts. All winter and spring he white-knuckled sobriety, hit those meetings at the church, and it landed him here — alone in a trailer at a landfill with his dog and the Quiet.

His whole life now a list of what not to do: Don't use. Don't drink. Don't hang out with people who drink, or go to places where people play music and drink, or take the calls from the West Coast in the middle of the night (even when you hear her Kim Carnes voice sobbing into the answering machine).

FIVE

The Turd

Indiana and Michigan: 1991–92

*D*URING MY FIRST WEEK BACK, I got a job at a local restaurant known far and wide as the Buffy. If I got a job, my parents told me, perhaps I could get a car. I earned my license first thing, practicing on the Honda, which was cake. A glorified go-cart.

Matthew lived like a feral animal by then, his appearances random as the family of possums that lived in the thicket of trees behind our house. He'd waltz into the kitchen at an odd hour, drink half a gallon of milk straight out of a jug, pocket a Coors Light and some beef jerky, and move on without a hello or good-bye.

He'd quit Arvin, though he still rented a room in a house and worked a new job as a line cook at a Mexican restaurant in the mall. Our parents had spent the year trying to help him get a life plan, a notion that didn't interest him. His only proposal was bounty hunter school in Arizona. He asked my folks to pay his tuition, travel, and living expenses so that he could study the art of tracking down criminals in exchange for money. When our parents refused, he accused them of sending me to a fancy school while denying him his own dreams. Matthew was talented, no doubt, but we all saw he lacked commitment and endurance.

Still, Mom felt bad about the whole thing. On her own, she sorted through the artwork Matthew left behind when he moved out. She had the best pieces matted and collected into a portfolio, which she took up to the prestigious Herron School of Art in Indianapolis. They accepted him, and our parents agreed to pay what tuition they could and help him get loans for the rest. Faced with a real option, Matthew quietly brushed it off. He wouldn't go.

Perhaps he felt caught between two worlds, same as I did. We were coloring outside the lines of what passed for a normal life, not as an act of rebellion, but because we couldn't see the lines in the first place.

Approaching adulthood did little to ease my desire to be included in my brother's affairs. I simply learned to mask my wants. They stank of vulnerability — a teenager's nightmare. So Matthew and I entered a phase of loose acknowledgment. If he didn't say hello, I wouldn't either. I'd sit at the kitchen table as he foraged for food. Careful to appear engrossed in a book, I'd note every detail with my peripheral vision: his jean jacket, Misfits T-shirt, bandanna tied Little Steven–style around his head, sunburn peeling at the nape of the neck. If he said something, I'd offer vague agreement. It was a dance, like trying to negotiate with the pack's alpha: only by refusing to look him in the eye did I stand a chance of finding my way in.

This charade, of course, did not cure my loneliness. I worked at the Buffy, taking orders from people who rarely acknowledged me unless they were issuing a complaint (which happened often, as my mind was too clouded to juggle multiple orders). At home, I read books, listened to music, and smoked cigarettes and drank

Mom's wine coolers on the front steps of the house. My parents didn't seem to notice. In their minds, I was home, so there was no reason to worry the way they often did when I was away.

One evening, the phone rang and I answered, lifting the yellow receiver out of Snoopy's paw (the phone an artifact from a childhood long gone).

"Matt home?" The thin, slow voice I recognized as Brad Atkins — Matthew's longtime friend — a brain-damaged, twenty-something divorced father of two. Matthew had lived for a stretch that year in Brad's ex-wife's attic.

"No. He's living somewhere else."

"You know where?"

"Those pink apartments behind the library, I think."

"Right on. This Missy?"

"Melissa."

"You home from that school?"

"Yeah."

"You like it?"

"No."

Brad laughed. I lit a cigarette. We talked about all kinds of things — this shithole of a town, my brother, jobs, then Brad read me Frank Zappa lyrics with the word *pussy* in them and I threatened to hang up. He apologized. I knew better, but the phone line between us made our connection feel like play. Brad was the only person I knew who seemed more alone than I felt. By the end of the night, I'd spent four hours talking him out of suicide. The next day, Brad, who only had three fingers on one hand, called twelve times.

"Why is Brad Atkins calling you?" Mom asked.

I shrugged.

"Tell me." She used the voice normally reserved for handling salesmen and service people.

"He called for Matthew and was real sad so I talked to him some."

She shook her head at the lost cause of me and threatened to sic the cops on Brad.

Left with no way to reach me, Brad walked up to the drive-through window at the Buffy during my next shift and refused to leave without talking to me. Even when he kept quiet and followed the rules, people wanted to call the cops on him, which is the action my manager threatened. Eventually Brad loped back down Washington Street in the direction from which he'd come.

Matthew blew through home soon after, pale-faced and tight-shouldered as if bracing himself against sunlight.

"I talked to Brad," he said. "He won't bother you again." He looked up once, meeting my eyes sharply for a heartbeat. "And if he does, you tell me."

"Okay," I said. "Thanks."

I had to leave the room for fear he might see my smile. A tingling spread through my body, all the way to my toes. My brother had looked me in the eyes and promised to protect me, the same brother who, not so long ago, had chased me through the neighborhood while brandishing nunchucks.

I understood that my mother probably had words with Matthew. I understood it was a mess of my own making that I'd better not repeat. But he had come to my defense. As the weight of this gesture sank in, the flush in my cheeks made me a shade more visible, a ghost momentarily seen.

By the end of my third week at the Buffy, I'd saved three hundred dollars in tip money. Dad said he'd match my funds, which brought my car budget in at over half a grand. My father knew in that way he has of knowing things that, despite my cagey teenage ways, my world was too small. So we spent weekend mornings sipping coffee while circling ads in the local and the Indianapolis papers.

"We can go as far as Cincinnati or Louisville for the right deal," he told me after our first week of searching Columbus turned up nothing but an overpriced gray Honda with pink velour interior. When we climbed inside I said, "It's like a giant pink taco." And by *taco* I meant *vulva*. Plus, Mom drove a Honda the color of curdled milk, and I would not be like her.

Dad and I soon scouted out a rust-brown 1980 Toyota Corolla, a four-door sedan, automatic, with vinyl interior. It had maybe one hundred thousand miles on it, though mileage didn't mean much to me at sixteen. The fact that it ran meant everything. We took it for a spin. It cruised on the highway, idled smoothly at stoplights, and sailed seamlessly through town. The only issues were cosmetic: rust spots, dirty interior, some exterior dings. All the better for me — I didn't have to worry about ruining her with spilled coffee and dropped cigarettes.

They wanted five hundred. Dad snagged her for four hundred cash.

"Save the extra for repairs," he said, handing me the keys. "Come by before your mom goes to bed. She'll want to see it."

I thanked him and headed into the night, passing factories (Arvin, Cummins, Mariah's meatpacking plant), then Sap's Donut Mill (home of "the world's best-selling donut"), and stunning midcentury buildings designed by famous architects — buildings I could not yet recognize as beautiful. I drove past the old cemetery, past the two-story house on California Street that I had loved best, and parked three cigarettes later in front of the house scored in summer by the sound of bouncing tennis balls from the courts across the street. I cut the engine, left the cassette player running, and smoked one more cigarette before my mother came out. She circled the vehicle, stepping into the road, barefoot, with a glass of wine.

"How much?"

"Four hundred."

She raised her brows and nodded again. Her hesitation surprised me. The Corolla and her Honda Civic — though eight years apart in age — were the same kind of fuel-efficient foreign cars that had rendered the Volaré obsolete, though my car didn't feel like Mom's Honda. It had personality, a well-loved patina. It shined.

Mom nodded in vague approval, but I could tell from the thin line her lips made that she didn't approve. Perhaps she felt strong-armed into helping me buy a car that would render me a sovereign nation, free to roam. Perhaps she noticed the ease of my hand on the wheel, a smoke in the other. My movements revealed a confidence I would not find again until I cradled my hours-old son in one hand while walking around the hospital room as if we'd been living in tandem my whole life, his body an extension of my own.

When Matthew saw my car a few days later, he put on his biggest grin as he circled her, pointing out things he liked. He climbed into the passenger's seat and I sat behind the wheel.

"Whatcha gonna call her?" he asked.

The idea of naming her had not occurred to me.

"I gotta say, she looks like a giant turd."

He punctuated this observation with his toothiest smile. His voice held such delight and reverence that a rare kind of gratitude overcame me, and I never once took the Turd for granted.

My brother became a constant source of worry for my parents. He partied after his kitchen shifts at La Bamba's, where he'd met a slightly older gal named Kim. Kim was a droopy-eyed hippie with a gentleness about her that I liked. More important, she was twenty-one. She could waltz into a liquor store and buy whatever she wanted, straight-up legal.

Somewhere in that stretch of time, Matthew got a minor-in-possession citation for wandering the streets with a Solo cup of booze. A few weeks later, he ran a four-way stop and fender-bumped another car. The Volaré came out with barely a scratch. The elderly driver of the other vehicle was rattled but unharmed. Still, Matthew felt terrible about it. Then he got arrested for drunk driving, earning him our mother's rage and three days in Columbus's brand-new jail. She dropped him from the family car insurance policy, and the Volaré got benched for the rest of the season. I learned most of this from listening to my mother talk to her friends when they met in our basement for drinks and smokes, right outside my bedroom door.

A few days after his release, Matthew shared with me one detail from his time in jail.

"Missy," he said, "we rolled asshole-smuggled tobacco in pages of the Bible. It was the best smoke I ever had." This was Matthew in his element. He loved convicts and sanitation workers the way I loved Flannery O'Connor and her peacocks. It was the start of our new relationship: he played muse, bringing me stories from a world I could not inhabit, and I would write them.

I tested this story on select Buffy co-workers, adding a little of this, a little of that, but never did I have to lie. The trick rested in making the true story of my brother believable. I could hardly wait to return to boarding school, where I would tell and tell and tell it.

The week before I left for school, Matthew showed up around midnight in our parents' kitchen. At night his body moved with a comfort it didn't have during the day. I sat in the breakfast booth watching MTV and trying to ignore him. This time I couldn't.

"I'm leaving next week." My voice cracked on arrival, so unsure I was of myself, of how to talk to him.

Matthew turned toward me and let the fridge door swing shut.

"You got a haircut," he said, as if remembering me in general.

"I did." I touched my new ear-length bob, inspired by a character on the television show *China Beach*. In seventh grade I'd had the *Dirty Dancing* cut and perm. By next year, I'd make the leap to a pixie style inspired by another show: *Northern Exposure*.

"Well, cool. You psyched to go back? You like it up there?"

"Better than here."

He smiled. "Yeah, I bet. I'm going to Vincennes, I figure."

In the latest turn of events, Matthew and my folks had compromised on a plan for his future: vocational school.

"Mom said. Airplane mechanics?"

"Yep."

We chatted about nothing in particular for a handful of minutes, like a couple of friends. It was the first real conversation we'd had in our new skins. We were shape-shifters, revisions of ourselves, barely recognizable as the kids in the Sears portraits hanging on the dining room wall.

Matthew grabbed some cans of Spam from the pantry, a block of Velveeta, a loaf of Wonder Bread, and slipped out the back door. I felt happy and sad watching him go.

But that's not why I'm telling you about that summer. I'm telling you because I loved that car. I grabbed on to it like a life raft, and it anchored me against the undertow of being a gullible, self-loathing sixteen-year-old girl in a town I never understood, a place I could never call home.

The drive from Columbus to Interlochen was the first solo road trip of my life. I loaded up the Turd with vintage lamps, a quilt Mamaw made for me, a carpet wall hanging of *The Last Supper,* and a guinea pig (which I smuggled into my dorm room). Mom let me drive myself on the condition I stop for the night near the Michigan-Indiana border and call home at the end of each day.

The stretch from Columbus to Indianapolis was old hat. I skipped the bypass and took I-65 straight through the downtown spaghetti bowl. Near Chicago, I turned north and checked in to a hotel, went for a swim, and watched television until I fell asleep. In the morning, I hit the road again, happy to see Lake Michigan, which looked as blue and wide as an ocean to me. I stopped on the shore for a stretch in Muskegon, read poems, re-upped my coffee, and motored on. On the road, I was no one's daughter, no one's student, no one's little sister, which made me feel more *me* than ever. A somber mood overcame me as I passed through Traverse City and coasted on fumes the final fifteen miles to Interlochen. I loved my school, but I loved the road more.

I parked the Turd on campus and turned over the keys to the dorm staff — we weren't allowed to drive at all while school was in session. I began my junior year at racecar pace and never slowed down. I wrote poems as fast as an Indianapolis 500 driver in time trials. When school was out of session, I gave my pen a rest and drove.

I took the Turd to Chicago, Ann Arbor, Boston, New York City even. Each break I'd find a friend to go along, or give a friend a ride home to Ohio, then drive to another friend's house in Wisconsin. After weeks on the road, I'd coast back to school, energized, alive, a person at the beginning of something. I couldn't figure out why this kind of travel drained people like Mom and Matthew but left me fully charged. I loved the anonymity, the autonomy, and people-watching strangers in strange lands. As soon as I arrived back at school, I studied maps, plotting my future in road trips.

Between adventures, I'd return to Indiana for a few days to appease my mother, but she couldn't hold me. I wasn't trying to be defiant. Communicating with her simply felt like shouting back and forth down a long, dark hallway.

I'd often space out on road trips and forget to call home. By the time I did remember — a day or three late — my mother was wrecked, her voice part plea, part yell.

"I called the state police to look for you. I had no idea if you were dead or not. Would you please call home? Please?"

"Sorry. I forgot."

I was always forgetting her, my indifference an unshakable chill in her heart (for reasons I would not understand until I had children of my own). But motion wasn't a choice for me. It was a calling. My legs twitched at night, propped on volumes of poetry in my dorm bed. I was hungry for the world, words, the back roads and highways of every known state. Uncharted forests and urban jungles and the strangers they held pulled at my imagination with a gravity I chose not to fight. To turn my back on that was to pour myself into the Jell-O mold of my parents' midwestern existence — something that held for me a potentially lethal dose of monotony.

After the summer spent waiting tables at the Buffy, a door cracked open between Matthew and me. He started sending me the occasional letter. Or envelope. (Calling them letters isn't quite accurate.) Every few months he sent a Polaroid of the toilet bowl featuring some bowel movement he found particularly fascinating, a tape measure pulled across the seat. The notes on the back offered a quick *Hi how are you?* and an observation about the object of the photo, such as *It looks like a seal,* or *Better than a foot-long* (and by "foot-long," I knew he meant the Dairy Queen hot dogs we loved as kids).

I kept these photos in an envelope next to my Brother word processor and soon had an entire collection. They were teenage poop jokes that returned us to the days of the Squareback, a time when every *poop* utterance made us laugh until we had to pee. The Polaroids, I understood, were peace offerings, olive branches, Matthew's way of calling a truce on the unspoken conflicts that had divided us.

I told stories at boarding school almost as often as I wrote them. My shy ways left me isolated and lonely. I moved like a ballerina, read Rilke in my spare time, and spoke only in small and familiar groups where I could command attention by slipping in an off-color story about my family. Like the time my algebra study partner noticed one of the toilet bowl pictures lingering on my desktop.

She pointed at the Polaroid but did not touch it.

"Oh, yeah. My brother sent that." I held up another photo in which my six-foot brother resembled both Sean Penn and Keanu Reeves. "This is him."

"That's *your* brother? He's so hot. And he sent you *that?*" She pointed again to the Polaroid.

I tried never to force a story, but when a door opened up, I'd step through it. I told her about one of Matthew's escapades involving a convenience store, poop smeared under a car door handle, and a dead iguana.

"Oh my god," she said when I got to the end. "Oh my god." She could hardly stop laughing.

We finally cracked our algebra texts and my study partner paused to ask a last question. "So you guys are close?"

Her words stopped me. I did my best to keep my mouth from hanging open. Matthew and I were biologically closer to each other than any other beings on this planet, yet our connection felt as nebulous as the dark side of the moon. My stories were balm on a wound too close for me to see: that my brother's answer to that question was *no*.

I became Matthew's walking archive to forge that closeness, a Greek chorus of one. He was an unending narrative full of twists and turns I could never dream up on my own. So I told those stories everywhere, to everyone.

Like this. Like I'm telling you now.

During the summer connecting my junior year to my senior, my last in Indiana, I bought some brown-tinted car wax and polished up the Turd, hiding her dings and rust spots as best I could. Her brakes had worn out and Dad suggested I upgrade instead of fixing her. We were having a garage sale. In black marker I wrote the price on a piece of cardboard and below that a too-long list of details:

> *22–25 mpg in town, up to 35 on the highway*
> *new stereo!*
> *manual*
> *power steering*
> *new rear passenger's wheel caliper*
> *ok tires*
> *comfortable seats*
> *needs new front brake pads*
> *best car ever*
> *driven 20,000 miles in just one year!*

In hindsight, it feels like I drove that car for an abbreviated lifetime. The slick brown plastic of the steering wheel underhand, the cigarette sculpture in the ashtray, the smell of vinyl and dust, all imprinted as deep in my brain as the scent of my mother's hand lotion.

I sipped coffee at that garage sale for about an hour before a determined-looking man my Papaw's age walked up to the the Turd, looked her over for less than a minute, and handed me five Ben Franklins — one hundred more than we'd paid for her — no questions asked.

"She's a great car," I said.

He nodded, friendly but not smiling.

I could tell he was the one who would keep her going for the long haul, and it made the goodbye a touch easier. He slid the front seat back, removed my cardboard love letter from the windshield, fired her up, and disappeared.

August 6, 2000

Nine shots in he starts calling people. He calls the girl from AA he hooked up with last winter who tried real hard to help. Tries still. She can hear the liquor in him but comes over anyway.

She drinks a Diet Coke, holds one of his hands, and her dark eyes turn sad over him.

Take Early, *he says. He picks up the blue heeler and hugs the dog till he growls.* He always liked you. Take him.

She will not take the dog. She pours him water, puts him to bed though it is only two, and says, There is nothing you can do you ever have to be ashamed of with me. I'll call tomorrow. We'll go to a meeting.

He calls Krista with the red pigtails, the one he should have married but then blew it up instead. She comes for a while, listens to that Lucinda Williams song he can't get enough of, then tells him to ditch the shots and leaves for work.

He calls Deuce — one of his best friends from way back. He calls again, but there's no answer. Deuce, he knows, is sick of his shit.

All day he calls Randy. Things can't end without Randy. He calls over and over, leaving messages, doing shots in between.

He tries hard not to but can't help thinking about his sister. She has this thing about her like a skittish dog, though he never could figure out what it was that hit her. She's hard to coax out, but when you get close it's the real deal. She's fine, though. Independent. Grown and married. He's kept every word she ever sent him.

He plays Lucinda again to drown out the Quiet.

I just stand with this glass in my hand feelin' like nothing even matters.

Louder. Louder. Songs. Women. A truck.

SIX

The Saab

Indiana, Michigan, and Montana: 1992–94

THE WEEKEND AFTER the garage sale, Dad and I drove his new-to-him Porsche 944 northwest, toward the Illinois state line, in pursuit of an '84 Saab 900. Dad had hoped I would adopt his Honda CRX, but the clutch was touchy and I hated the low-rider feel of it. So he sold the CRX and replaced it with his dream car — the same red Porsche that Jake Ryan drove in the movie *Sixteen Candles*. I didn't care one lick for the Porsche, but the Saab intrigued me. It was a sedan-size hatchback — like some bastard offspring of the Turd and a Squareback.

I'd already landed a job bagging groceries for the summer at the Kroger. I'd also shaved my head and bought blue-tinted Sinéad O'Connor glasses. I got some strange looks from patrons, but everyone pretty much left me alone. I'd opted for grocery bagging instead of waiting tables again so that I would have the mental space to daydream, write poems, and become a proper misanthrope. A quirky import like the Saab seemed an ideal accessory for my artistic alienation.

Shortly after passing through the small town of Greencastle, we pulled down a dirt drive onto a farm. The owner was a divorced engineer and swore by the Saab's design. He sold me on her quirks instantly: the hood opened backwards, the engine was installed backwards, and the front windshield was as large and round as a bay window, much like the seventies VW camper vans. The rear seats folded down to make a space long enough for sleeping, and the interior was a burgundy velour that reminded me of Mamaw and Papaw's New Yorker. This was a Swedish vehicle, the owner explained, with valuable features for someone living up north, like the heated seats, which impressed me even though they no longer worked. Saab, he told me, had put out its first car just after World War II. The company, named using an acronym for Svenska Aeroplan Aktiebolaget, or Swedish Airplane Corporation, had designed planes to defend Sweden's sovereignty. Once the war ended, Saab started making cars.

Dad drove the Saab a mile or so away from the owner's house and turned it over to me on a deserted dirt road. New to a stick shift, I let up the clutch and coasted successfully in first. I shifted into second, then third. By the time I followed Dad home that evening, I could shift seamlessly through all the gears.

In the Saab I traveled north and eventually west. Her engine hummed most happily at exactly seventy-three miles per hour — her sweet spot. The two years that I owned her I spent almost entirely in Montana and Michigan, so busy exercising my freedom that Matthew and I rarely saw each other. The one time we managed to connect happened by default, when I gave him a ride to our great-grandmother's funeral.

Mary Cooper was my mother's grandmother, the one who gave my parents some cash to buy a car for a wedding gift. Our generations were close in age, so Grandma Cooper was only in her seventies when we were young. She was the only grandmother we had who acted much like a grandmother. Mamaw was too busy getting shit done to think about nurturing, and Betty—our mother's mother—focused so much on her own needs that she didn't feel much like a grandmother either. Grandma Cooper—Betty's mother—was the one who hosted Christmases, the one whose house we loved to stay in, the one I found sitting alone in her easy chair in the mornings, sipping coffee, and smiling like she'd been waiting for me. Not long after I left for Interlochen, Grandma Cooper suffered a stroke that left her half paralyzed. She never spoke again, never walked again, and during my senior year, she left her busted body behind for good.

I drove down from Interlochen in time for the viewing. The next day, Mom asked me to pick up Matthew in Vincennes, where he was in school for airplane mechanics, and bring him to the funeral. I'm not sure if he had the Volaré there or not, or if his license was suspended or not. Either way, his various arrests had put him off driving.

In his boarding house in Vincennes, he sat on his twin bed and gestured for me to take the chair.

"You like that car?" Matthew nodded his head toward the window.

"The hood opens backwards."

He stared at me like I might be fucking with him.

"It's Swedish," I explained. I told him a bit about Saab's aviation roots, struggling for connection between my car love and his vocation.

He laughed, propped an ankle on his knee, and rolled up his pant leg. Illegible letters circled his calf—a new tattoo. He had a rat on his chest already and some kind of totem up his spine.

He pulled a large flathead nail from his pocket, sparked a lighter, and heated the nail head over the flame.

"They had an open casket at the viewing," I told him. Our great-grandmother had looked like a wax version of herself. It was the first time I'd seen a vacated body, and it made me think about the meat section of a supermarket. "They put too much makeup on her. Or not enough."

Matthew looked up for a second. "Mom cry?"

"Yeah. Lots. Plus all the aunts."

He shook his head back and forth. "That's some fucked-up shit, right there."

He seared his leg tattoo with the glowing head of the nail. As he winced, I smelled burnt hair and skin.

"Doesn't that hurt?"

He shrugged.

"Why are you burning it?"

"Don't like it."

He let up on the nail and breathed deeply, like an athlete recovering from a dead lift. Some self-destructive streak was growing in him, manifesting in excessive tattoos, stories spun as funny when the truth is they were dangerous and often offensive. He even made a point to say words like *ain't,* dumbing-down his language on purpose for reasons I didn't understand.

"I'm never gonna die like that. All those ventilators and shit. If they'd just let her go when she had her stroke. Held a pillow over her head or something. That's what I'd want." The flame from his lighter reflected in his irises as he spoke.

"I only visited her once," I said. "She thought I was Aunt Lisa." Her mouth had opened and closed as she stared at me, gulping in air like a landlocked fish.

"I went too, but I didn't go in. Smelled like baby shit and bleach, even from the outside. Mom freaked out and I was like, 'Mama, whatever's in there ain't Grandma. And wherever Grandma is, she doesn't want me in there.' But Mom just kept on. You know how she gets."

He plunged the nail down again, next to the first spot. "If Dad ever dies I'll prolly buy a motorcycle and ride all over the country. That's what he wanted to do, but then got Mom pregnant."

Though our father was recently diagnosed with type 2 diabetes, his eventual death had never occurred to me. The thought of it brought to mind a passage from a Katherine Anne Porter short story I read in middle school, in which María Concepción rends her clothes and growls at the sky.

Matthew went back to heating up the nail.

"I worry about Mom," he said.

"What about Mom?" I asked. I couldn't handle much more death talk.

"She drinks. A lot." He plunged the nail down again and paused to inspect the string of burns.

It was the first time I heard him say it out loud, and it confirmed the reality no one acknowledged. Somewhere along the line we'd gone from the family with the mom everyone else wanted — the mom who tended every owwie and cooked all the food and took her daughter to every Broadway musical that came through Indy — to the family with the mom who started pouring Chardonnay at two, laughed too loud all evening long, and stumbled to bed by eight, drunk, without dinner.

"But I don't worry about Mom dying," Matthew said. "I worry more that she'll live to be a hundred and never stop being pissed." He smiled like he'd just delivered a punch line.

Matthew was right. Our mother spent most of her time in one of two modes: manic celebration and silent anger over unknown offenses. (It would take me years to figure out how to express my anger with words instead of averted eyes, loud sighs, and door slams.)

Matthew checked his look in a small mirror, slicked his hair back with some Royal Crown, and tucked his shirttails into his jeans — a first. We caught eyes in the mirror and he flashed me his best car-salesman grin. He'd changed so entirely with a single wink that I found no trace of myself left in his reflection.

"Let's go," he said.

Lanky and tall, he had to slide the passenger's seat of the Saab back to fit his legs inside. He looked like a man wedged into a clown car, and I was proud as hell to give him a ride. I let him pick the music, and he popped in a Grateful Dead cassette — our little secret, I understood, as our grandmother's funeral was no time for the Ramones or Suicidal Tendencies. I drove us down the small two-lane highways connecting Vincennes to the tiny town of Russellville (population 354) where our great-grandmother, Mary Cooper, had lived and died.

Other attempts to meet that year ended up a series of misfires. My entire family arrived for my graduation from Interlochen — a gathering so overwhelming that both Matthew and I would have run from it normally. Matthew drove up in the Volaré along with a friend from airplane mechanic school — a heavyset fella known simply as Roundman. For Matthew to drive this far required two things — the help of a friend, and a sincere desire to be there for me. I couldn't wait to show my big brother off to my friends who'd heard so many stories about him.

The mother of a classmate rented a house at a nearby ski resort, which became the official graduation party site. I gave Matthew and Roundman directions and headed over in the Saab. The place was swanky. Though my friends were there, all of us dressed in flannel shirts and old jeans, many wealthier, fancier kids were there too. I talked for a bit with David from Mexico, whose mother, I'd heard, was a well-known telenovela actress. He told me that his father (a film producer) had talked Gabriel García Márquez into writing one of his college recommendation letters. I sipped from a Mickey's forty-ouncer that outsized my head and kept waiting for Matthew to arrive. Finally Jesse, whose mother had rented the cabin, whistled to get everyone's attention. (Jesse was the kind of guy who looked really small in person but modeled for Calvin Klein as a summer job.) He asked if anyone knew the two dudes sitting on a cooler on the porch. He said that kind of thing *didn't look good*.

Outside I found Matthew and Roundman looking like they'd just pulled in from a Hells Angels rally. I couldn't have been happier to see them, but Matthew refused to come inside. He could hardly look me in the eye, actually, and I felt guilty—the source of his discomfort. He gave me a Guinness and congratulated me, but he would not join the rich-kid party. I went back inside to try to lure some of my friends out and returned to find Matthew, Roundman, and the Volaré gone.

By the time I left Interlochen, I'd turned in a senior portfolio more than two hundred pages long. My biggest cheerleader, Delp, flipped through the manuscript I'd slid across his desk.

"You've done more work than any student I've had," he said, catching my eye. "You know that?"

I looked away as I nodded, thrilled and embarrassed.

"Good. Now make sure you understand this: It's all practice. All of it." He shook my pages at me. "Every word. And you won't know until you're done writing when it's more. So consider it all practice, and never stop practicing. Right? Stephenson?"

"Right."

I knew what he was telling me, but I doubted myself capable of the kind of endurance I'd need to become a real writer. It could wait, I thought. I was a legal adult now with wheels of my own and a roll of graduation checks in my pocket.

. . .

In the fall of '93, I drove the Saab west to start college in Missoula, Montana. Most of my Interlochen friends had chosen small liberal arts colleges like Bennington, Oberlin, or Sarah Lawrence. Others went on to Ivy League schools or prestigious conservatory programs. I'd spent most of my senior year reading Jim Harrison and Hemingway. Using the Jungian concept of synchronicity passed down to me by my father, I let a series of coincidences guide my college choice. After reading three books in a row that made positive mentions of Missoula (*A River Runs Through It, For Whom the Bell Tolls,* and Harrison's *Legends of the Fall*), I applied to the University of Montana. I filled out applications for some private schools as well: Reed in Portland, Sarah Lawrence, and a small school in Vermont called Marlboro, chosen mostly because it was named after a brand of cigarettes. When I visited Missoula to check out U of M, I fell into a deep, immediate love for this town — a love that has never left me.

That's one true story I tell about how I came west, but there's another story buried inside, rarely told but just as true.

Though I didn't think twice about it back then, I'm certain I chose a less competitive college to stay connected to my Indiana roots. I eventually chose a graduate school in the same half-assed way — I missed the deadlines for the more prestigious places, applied to a random sampling of schools, and picked the least pretentious and most affordable option. I was willing to surpass the achievements of my family by going to college and grad school, but I would keep things real by not aiming too high. It's what some call a case of imposter syndrome, only my fear was not so much that I'd be discovered a fraud. It was more an allergy to places that felt fancy. Whether it was a restaurant with cloth napkins or a school for the elite, those places didn't feel like me any more than Mom's new Civic had felt like the Us I'd grown up believing in. I thrived on frayed clothing, blue highways, rivers with boulders the size of Volkswagens stranded midstream, and an approachable set of low expectations. But put me in the spotlight and I'll freeze.

This flight instinct is what got me into my first wreck, in part. I drove my new college boyfriend around Missoula one busy afternoon. His presence so flustered me that I miscalculated a left turn and we braced ourselves as a late-model SUV nailed the rear driver's side of the Saab. My folks' insurance covered the damages, but the Saab became riddled with electrical problems no mechanic seemed able to fix, so I did what came naturally to me — I avoided her.

In the summer of '94, I left the Saab in storage in Missoula and rode up to Alaska with a boy I didn't much get along with, mostly because I fell for his VW camper van, Tillie — a late-seventies bay-window model. Tillie had a steering wheel like you'd find on a school bus, an engine that sounded like a commercial sewing machine, and a couch in back that converted into a bed. She was the vehicle I'd been waiting for — a ride designed for questing and nesting. Though I loved riding in Tillie, she wasn't mine. Her owner and I argued all the way to Alaska and parted ways in Anchorage, where I set out on foot, alone — too proud to call my parents and ask for a plane ticket home.

Just south of town, a brown truck pulled over for me — my first ride. I took it as a good sign because the Turd and the Saab were brown and my shirt that day was brown and my middle name has always been Brown. Before I reached the pickup, the driver pushed the door open from the inside. He was round as a Santa, with a beard and donut ring of brown hair. He smiled and tipped an invisible hat to me. "Headin' south?"

He agreed to take me halfway to Homer, which is better than I expected from my first five minutes of hitchhiking solo in Alaska. (My first five minutes hitchhiking ever, in fact.)

"What's in Homer?" he said. His eyes cut away from the road and into me.

"Work."

"You got friends there?"

"Yes," I lied. I had no one but the boy I was mad at back in Anchorage, who did not expect to hear from me. A bad feeling started welling up inside me, but there was nothing I could think to do but ride along.

"Where you from?" He stretched an arm across the back of the bench seat behind me.

"Montana. I go to school there."

"You like Pantera?" He pushed a black cassette into the tape deck and bobbed his head up and down to the beat.

"I got my own music." I put on my headphones, but he kept trying to talk to me as I looked out the window to the horizon, where jagged pines pierced the never-dark sky. No road signs, no people. Just wild.

After a half-hour or so, he turned off the main road without explanation.

"Where you going?"

"Gotta take photos of an abandoned refinery. It's my job. It'll just take a little while, then we'll head back south."

"I can get out here. This is good." I watched the main road disappear behind us in the side-view.

"It ain't no problem, honey." Pantera screeched from the speakers as he reached for my hand. I pulled it into my lap, but he caught my wrist. "Come on — don't you want to be friends?"

"I'm fine," I said. It is all that came to me, a phrase my mother uses to say *Leave me alone* in the nicest possible way.

He kept hold like that as we rode, and I tried to memorize each turn he took on the back roads. We were in a valley: open fields cornered in by sharp mountains, their peaks far above tree line. The woods were my only chance. Then what?

He finally parked in a browned-out lot near some old towers and buildings. I noted the edge of my frame pack resting against the tailgate.

"Your stuff is safe, honey. Come on. Let me take your picture." He stepped in close with his camera, between the truck and me, shutter clicking.

"Why you lookin' like your mom died, girl? Come on. I give you a ride, you can give me a smile."

He kept coming closer, until he let the camera hang from his neck as he grabbed me in a headlock. I tried to back out of his grasp. When I couldn't, I beat on his back, kicked at his shins.

"Hey, now." He backed up an arm's length and we faced off like boxers. "I thought we was friends. I ain't gonna hurt you if you just come 'ere."

I grabbed my frame pack from the truck bed and waved it in front of me. In a dream, this is the part where I would fly, fleeing the scene by propelling my body mountain-high and into some better land. Instead, I told him the kinds of things I'd heard you're supposed to. My story came out fast and blurred.

"My name is Melissa and I'm from Columbus, Indiana, and I have a mother there and a father and a brother who love me and they would kick your ass if you hurt me because they are waiting for me and if you so much as fucking touch me again I will spend the rest of my days haunting your ass until the only wish you'll have at night, in the dark, in the winter, is that you'd never let me in your goddamn car."

He took a step back and held his hands up in surrender. "Whoa, girl. I didn't want to scare you. I mean, hell, I'm sorry. You're pretty and I thought —"

I strapped on my pack and started up the road in what I guessed was the right direction. He followed me in his truck with the window rolled down, talking the whole while. I think his eyes were even wet. After two miles, I made him agree to let me drive. He rode in back and let me take him a hundred miles out of his way to my destination. By midnight, we'd made it to Homer. I drove us all the way out to the spit where the wind ripped against the tents of the sleeping cannery workers.

"Here," he said. He handed me three twenties. "Really, I'm sorry."

With the help of two guys, I pitched my tent on the beach and afterward listened to them dare each other to unzip my door. I ate my only food — a jar of peanut butter — and drank all my water. I stayed up all night, my only knife clenched in my fist.

I hitched back to Anchorage the next day, lucky for one good ride straight to the airport. I used every last bill for a flight to Seattle, then a Greyhound to Missoula, where I busted the Saab out of storage. She ran dream-smooth for thirty-six hours straight, through South Dakota, Minnesota, Wisconsin, Chicago, and Indy — all the way to my parents' front door.

"What happened to Alaska?" Mom asked.

"It was pretty, but no work." I reeked of cigarettes and gas station coffee, my hair windblown halfway to dreadlocks.

She poured me some tea and herself some wine and we sat together in her Christmas-colored kitchen watching helicopter views of O.J. Simpson's white SUV caught in a slow-motion chase on the highways of Los Angeles. I imagined the football star strapped in his seat with no future but the six lanes of vacant highway before him and a partial tank of gas. I needed to eat, shower, and sleep, but I couldn't turn the live footage off until the

car chase came to an end. Guilty or innocent, I just wanted him
out.

I went back to work a final summer at Interlochen and sold the
Saab to Delp, who planned to use it as his fishing rig. At my request, Dad scouted a 1984 Volkswagen Vanagon. This was a newer
version of the bus that had taken me to Alaska, and her metallic
brown paint shimmered in the sun. She'd clocked only fifty-five
thousand miles in her decade of life. On our test drive, she coasted
in town and on the highway smooth as a shuttle in orbit. She was a
tin-top passenger van instead of a Westfalia like Tillie, but she was
mine. I drove her back to Montana for good. No more summers in
Michigan.

Around the same time, Matthew graduated with honors from
his program in Vincennes. While the architecture of flight came
easily to him, the practice did not. With his degree in hand, he
walked away from employment in the field and headed south, to
Athens, Georgia, with a few other Indiana boys who were dear
friends of his. In preparation for his biggest migration yet — one
that would actually stick — he let the Volaré go. By then, she was an
art car of sorts — sky blue with a dozen gunshot holes in her sides,
which Matthew had turned into the bodies of black-winged birds.
Behind them? Spray-painted clouds. He sold her to an ex-girlfriend, who took her west, to college in Washington State.

Matthew and I became the first members of our extended family to attempt life beyond Indiana state lines, which made us or-
phans of sorts, transplants, grown-up runaways, more sure of
what we weren't than who we were. We didn't belong where we'd
come from, and we had no roots where we'd landed. Matthew used
friends and a breakout music scene to anchor him. The van was my
glitter and glue — I loved it, and it stuck. I had no need to upgrade.

The week I turned twenty-one, I went to a bar and met a bright-eyed, dark-haired boy named Joshua. He moved in. We went camping, drove the van around the country, graduated college, and landed jobs.

We got one dog. Then another. We got engaged. We got hitched. And I got lost.

August 6, 2000

When he drinks, there's company. Longtime loves and beautiful strangers, best friends, new friends. He can make anyone laugh.

I bet you, man, I bet I can make that girl more beautiful. Just watch.

And he did it, with a wisp of a woman who wore her hair over her face and arms crossed over her heart. It wasn't a game. He has an instinct for finding what shines in others and drawing it out. It's more sacred than anything he ever saw in church.

What exactly is he supposed to do? Road trip across the country, like his sister? He loves cars but would rather ride shotgun than drive — choose the music, light smokes. Keeping people company is what he's always done best, and now he's supposed to sit still and breathe? Like a monk counting to ten again and again and again?

The music stops, and the Quiet returns, amplified. He won't. Can't.

Another cassette in the deck, and three more shots down the hatch: for the father, son, and Holy Spirit.

Part 2

SEVEN

U-Haul

Montana: July, 2000

*T*WO DAYS BEFORE MY BROTHER'S twenty-ninth birthday, on a late-July Sunday in Missoula, Montana, my husband and I load the contents of our lives into a U-Haul. Beyond all reason, we are Texas bound. Josh carries a military backpack stuffed with books, poster tubes in hand. The son of a logger and a high school cheerleader now deceased, he has lived his whole life in this town. His wrists are thick as tree branches, and his deep-set eyes can go from compassion to irritation with a shift in the angle of his brows. He is the charming, dynamic half of our partnership — a light as bright as my mother or brother.

He is also the most intelligent, goodhearted, and attractive man to ever pay me attention. We first spotted each other the month I moved to Montana. I saw him talking to friends on the steps of the student union. He had so many friends, and a pair of smart-looking horn-rimmed glasses. But he didn't smoke. He glanced back as I lit up. I looked around to find out what he was staring at, only to discover it was me. Embarrassed to the core, I lowered my head and rushed off. A month or a year later I spied him again — surrounded

by friends, not smoking, staring — and I ran. I guessed by then he
thought me affected, or indifferent at best. Either way, the sight of
him both attracted and mortified me. Another year later I ran into
him on the street outside the restaurant where I worked. I was carrying a full tray of hot coffees and wore a linen apron stained gray
at the belly from washing dishes. I answered his offer to help with
a knee-jerk *no* while opening the restaurant door with my foot and
shimmying my way inside — escaping him again.

The week I turned twenty-one I went to a bar for the first time
in my life, with my restaurant friends. I didn't yet drink much
(aside from occasional binge-drinking in my teens), and I'd just
quit smoking for the first time, so I wasn't quite sure what to do
with myself. Then I saw him through the smoke, across the bar, sitting pint in hand, people-watching. I told my girlfriend the story
of him (that was not yet a story of us), then swore her to secrecy.
A half-hour later I caught sight of her pulling on his shirtsleeve
and pointing to me as if begging. My friends made a human corral
to keep me from doing the one thing I know to do: run. I'd almost
teared up from shame by the time he stepped into the ring, grazed
my elbow with his fingers, and said, *Hey.*

He calmed me with a single word. *Hey,* he said, *would you like a
smoke?* I accepted, my no-smoking resolve abandoned. We started
talking and kept going for hours, days, weeks, and years. In the fall
of 1999 we married, on October 17 — my twenty-fifth birthday.

Now he's moving to Texas because he doesn't want to lose me.
Though he won't yet see this journey for what it is (a step toward
a better life, I hope), he sees how happy it makes me to prepare for
a road trip, even a migration as logistically complex as this one. I
can't hide the pleasure I get from packing a suitcase or studying a
map.

Though I worry he will wake up one day and decide I'm a mistake, and that this move might trigger such a revelation, I have

to leave Montana. Not long ago I got a call from a National Book Award–winning author. He was pleased to inform me that I'd been accepted into the creative writing master's program at Texas State University, where he taught. He mumbled some generic praise to let me know that while he'd not taken the time to personally read my short stories, he had faith in the opinion of the man who did. I recognized the shock-and-awe strategy, but I didn't mind. The program director took over, congratulating me on earning a top scholarship to the graduate writing program, and a teaching position, should I want to come south to San Marcos, Texas.

There was no decision to be weighed. What other people saw as choice or accident I secretly considered divine intervention. My entire being answered *yes yes yes*. I told Josh the good news. He reeled, but we quit our jobs, emptied the house for the new owners, and loaded up this U-Haul together. All because *I had a feeling.*

Once the last box is taped shut and loaded, we sit for a last time on the front porch. I attempt to raise my husband's spirits by engaging him in song. *"The stars at night are big and bright"* — clap clap clap clap — *"deep in the heart of Texas."*

He shoots a brief smile — an expression picked up and discarded.

"Here," he says, handing me a smoke like it's the night we met all over again.

The sun hangs high in the cloudless sky, Mount Jumbo and Mount Sentinel glowing gold in the background as our dogs play in the yard. Missoula is my adopted home, but I know I have to learn more places before I can stay.

On this drive, I'll add three new states to my list of thirty-two visited. I have lived in Indiana, Michigan, and Montana; driven I-90 from Boston to Seattle; and traversed the Midwest so often that a log of my routes would look like a piece of my mother's seventies string-and-nail art, but I have never set foot in Colorado, New Mexico, or Texas.

I take a long last drag. "Ready?"

"I guess." Josh shrugs as he says this, eyes fixed on the house.

I give him a kiss and his shoulders unclench.

"Ready," he says.

I close the U-Haul door then load the dogs into my Volkswagen van. We drive back to the rental place, where they attach the tow apparatus to the U-Haul hitch. This will be the first road trip I've taken where my van gets a lift instead of giving me a lift.

Back home for the last time, I tranquilize the dogs. The blue heeler rides in the U-Haul next to Josh. My gentle giant — a shepherd-malamute rescue dog — stretches out in the backseat of my mother's '88 Honda Civic — a gift she gave us last spring.

We pull onto I-90 — me in the Honda following Josh in the U-Haul. As we enter Hellgate Canyon — named after Native American ambushes staged over a century ago — I focus on the round headlights of the VW in front of me. Missoula shrinks in the rearview until all I can see is the canyon, the interstate before us, the sun shining down on the mountains flanking the road — Sapphire range on the right, Garnets to the left. The van pulls me forward — her flat face magnetized to my heart.

I pick up a walkie-talkie and press the orange bar on the side.

"Thar she goes," I say. The mountains swallow the valley behind us.

Radio silence.

"You copy?"

"Roger that."

I calm myself by cataloging the automobiles passing by, the older models among them prompting involuntary smiles: a VW bug, a beat-to-hell Aries K, and best of all a sixties Ford Ranchero

— a rare kind of car with a truck bed and the low suspension of a sedan, cousin of the El Camino.

The only Bible verse I've ever committed to heart comes to mind, Ruth 1:16: *And Ruth said, Intreat me not to leave thee, or to return from following after thee: for whither thou goest, I will go; and where thou lodgest, I will lodge: Thy people shall be my people, and thy God my God.* I suggested using this in our wedding vows last fall. Not much of the Bible reached me, but the story of Ruth and Naomi did — Ruth's loyalty as bright in my imagination as New York City once was. But Josh had taken a class on Friedrich Nietzsche and felt strongly about incorporating the concept of the Eternal Return into our vows. I agreed in part because the language we used came from one of my favorite novels: *The Unbearable Lightness of Being* by Milan Kundera. Also, I wanted Josh to feel some ownership in our mutual destiny. The eternal return would give our union weight, the idea being that we will marry over and over in some universal loop in which every choice we make has gravity because we will make it again and again and again forever. So I said yes, and I held his hand and said yes, and he kissed me and said yes, and we meant it.

As the golden grasses and dark pines of southern Montana rise and fall around me, I don't yet know how hard Josh will take being separated from his home state. I can't know, really. I am a Hoosier, raised in a place known for flat highways, cornfields, racecars, basketball, and racism. Anywhere but there has always felt like improvement.

I do know that Texas is closer to Georgia than Montana, that Matthew's more likely to visit since we'll live on the outskirts of Austin and he's a live-music lover to the core. Slowly, my brother and I are coming back together on this continent. I have dim dreams that maybe one day we will be neighbors, help raise each other's children, and enjoy each other in a way we never could in the house where we grew up.

On our fourth and last day on the road, we bypass Austin, taking Highway 12 — a shoulderless two-lane — through the Texas Hill Country, former home to Lyndon B. Johnson, current home to tarantulas, rattlesnakes, scorpions, and cedar trees. It feels like the scene of an ambush in an old Western. The sun burns seat belt lines into my shoulder through the Civic window. Josh calls me on the walkie-talkie:

"My wheels on the road?"

"Yeah, barely."

It seems only by some act of magic that the U-Haul stays in our lane. We sway and correct, sway and correct until finally our little caravan pulls into San Marcos, where we coast through the quiet, darkening neighborhood and into the driveway of our new house.

Inside, we find a cold bottle of champagne — a gift from our realtor. We pop the cork on the back deck and take turns drinking from the bottle. Night falls and we discover that even in the darkest hours the air in these parts rarely dips below eighty in summer. The blue heeler snaps a giant tree roach out of the air and drops it at our feet. It is a couple inches long with an amber exoskeleton. The roach still moves, and I step on it, the remains reminding me of peppered cottage cheese.

"It's a good little house." Josh puts on the half-smile that still gives me butterflies.

"We're going to be fine. I'll go to school, you can figure out what you want to do, play music, and then we can stay here, go back to Montana, go somewhere else — whatever we want."

"Yeah."

"We can go back," I tell him. "I promise."

"Okay."

We drag the mattress from the van, bending it like a taco to fit through the doorway. Even with the AC on full blast, it's too hot to sleep under a sheet. Throughout the night, nails scrape against hardwood as the dogs wake, disoriented, to survey the boundaries of their new den.

We rest after so many miles, our bodies adjusting to the stillness, my skin buzzing from the road. One sleep before we wake to a new life in San Marcos, Texas, population 34,733 + 2, zip code: 78666.

August 6, 2000

Hit me, *he says.* Come on, man, just hit me.

Randy is the last Sunday visitor.

I ain't gonna hit you, Matt. Cut that shit out.

Randy goes in for a hug but Matthew won't have it. He starts pushing. Crying, spitting. Hit me fucking hit me you pussy.

Randy tackles him at the waist so he falls into the recliner. He goes down easy, stays down, barely conscious until he wakes in bed to the sound of Randy's engine. His brain cut out, is all — vodka-soaked synapses sparking and snuffing, an engine flooded.

He stumbles to the kitchen window to call Randy back, but it's too late. He can't be alone like this. Only five-thirty now and the sun still high, the world a smeared painting. No one left to call but his family — he can't.

He knows the second Randy's engine fades he'll be left with the deafening nothing and nobody to hold on to.

But wait. Here. Here's something. Something firm and real and familiar. Grab on now before it happens, before the last sound goes, before the Quiet —

EIGHT

Subway Car 66

Texas: August 2000

*A*UGUST COMES TO TEXAS just after we do. The sun rises each morning, the highs soaring into the triple digits — 110, 111, 113. The humidity seals the heat in for the night and turns me into a curly-haired girl for the first time in my life. There is no good time to be outside, among the banana spiders, black widows, fire ants, scorpions, and feral cats. The dogs pace the length of our two-bedroom bungalow, wanting out for a walk and wanting back in minutes later. The San Marcos River runs through town, coming within a block of our house, though the sluggish waters are a distant cousin to the swift Montana rivers I've come to know: the Blackfoot, the Clearwater, the Bitterroot. Even the polluted Clark Fork that bisects Missoula is majestic in comparison. Every time I think about dipping more than a toe into the San Marcos River, a scene from the Larry McMurtry novel *Lonesome Dove* comes to mind: While driving cattle across a Texas river, a horse steps on a nest of water moccasins and the young rider falls in and dies with a dozen snakes attached to his face. It's a scene my mother used to replay over and over, thrilled by the spectacle of it.

No fucking thank you.

I begin to wonder what I've done by bringing us here, to a time and place so deeply uncomfortable. In the mornings, I walk the dogs to the river for swim. On our first visit, a cat-size rodent crawls onto a log and watches us. I find out later the locals call this creature a "river rat." Known officially as nutrias, they have long skinny tails and fat brown bodies, and thrive in the tall grasses on the banks, cooling themselves in the shallows during the hottest hours. They're the kind of animal one might invent to populate a futuristic cautionary tale, though I can't help but think of them as Manny Rat — the nightmare nemesis who haunted my dreams as a child. I'd seen Manny Rat in an animated movie about a pair of wind-up mice — father and son — who fell into the trash at the toy store and got lost in a landfill. They met Manny Rat in the dump, and he hunted them down in the movie the way he hunted down my mother in my dreams. Always, he killed her. Always, I couldn't stop him.

The dogs' barking has no effect on the nutria. It stares back, un-afraid.

It is two weeks before school starts, and six weeks before the first paycheck from my position as a teaching assistant arrives. Josh searches the classified ads while I arrange the furniture, set up the kitchen, and connect the cable. On our sixth day in Texas, I decide to soothe us by creating a new marital ritual: Sunday dinner and television shows — something we rarely do together since we've been working weekends in caregiving facilities for two years.

I brave the strange new grocery store — HEB — and buy salmon, sweet potatoes, and salad fixins. By early evening, I begin cooking, broiling the potatoes and salmon. The temperature inside passes eighty though the air conditioner runs full blast. It will take an-other year for me to learn that ovens are seasonal tools in the south, best left dormant until winter.

We sit down to watch my favorite show, our skin sticking to the furniture, bare feet to the wood floors. I crack two Coronas, pop in some limes, and bring us steaming plates of food to eat in the living room as *The X-Files* begins. I look to Josh and we hum along to the theme song together — *do do do do do dooo...* It's one of those things we do that always makes me laugh, but not tonight.

I try, but I can't stomach the fish. It is pale and slimy and gigantic — a farm-raised monster breed I am not yet familiar with. Even an extra lime squeezed on top can't make it right. I eat little, slam three beers. Near the climax of the show, the phone rings. Josh walks into the back hallway as he answers. His tone makes the hair on my arms stand up. I put down my drink, turn off the television, and listen to an un-sound, an absence, a black hole opening, gravity shifting.

It is the silence of time breaking.

As he rounds the corner, his gaze meets mine — face heavy, mouth ajar. He looks away and holds out the phone, confirming my instinct: a bad thing has happened. Some wrong and unchangeable thing. I stand, step backwards. Josh apologizes as he presses the receiver into my hand.

My mother wails in the background.

My father lets loose the simple words: "Matthew shot himself in the head."

He shot himself in the head.

Shot himself.

In the head.

There is a tone in my father's voice — a finality. My brother is dead. Done. Gone.

I want to drop the phone, rewind the tape, drive every mile of highway back to Montana in reverse. Instead, I search for words to soothe my parents (the same words I will use a decade later when I tell my kids their father has moved states away, for good): "It's not your fault. It's not your fault. Not your fault. Not your fault."

After the call, I sit on the steps of the deck, barefoot on splintering wood. My brain fights the facts: Matthew died at five-thirty this evening of a self-inflicted gunshot wound. August sixth. My mind fires questions without answers:

What kind of gun?

I don't know.

Was he using?

I don't know.

Drunk?

Probably.

Was there a girl involved?

I'm sure.

Did he leave a note?

I don't know.

Why would he do that?

I do not know.

Didn't he love you?

I don't fucking know.

But I do know what it's like to want to leave the world. I do know the despair, the sadness, the urge to fall down the rabbit hole of the self until the problem with you is you and nothing feels good anymore and even your sleep becomes haunted. Shark dreams — a phrase Matthew coined after the movie *Jaws* gave him nightmares. As an adult, I took his talk of shark dreams as a sign of plagued sleep. I know that feeling. I had Manny Rat, after all. But I thought he understood that such darkness passes like weather. I thought he knew that there's a trapdoor at the bottom of every rabbit hole. On the other side of the door, a favorite song on the radio, or a beer on a hot day, or some beautiful human who makes you want to do better, aim higher. I thought he knew that you might slash tires or shoot up cars, but you never ever aim at yourself. I'd learned that lesson after two small cuts on my arm led to a year of deep sleep, isolation, and Ritalin.

Josh sits beside me, wraps an arm around my shoulders. "I'm so fucking sorry, babe."

I ask for vodka and a cigarette. I open my mouth to speak a few times, but my face wrenches up as the tectonic plates of my being grind and split. My molecules reel against a world without my brother. It's an emotional big bang, shrapnel spinning off to form planets it will take me years to discover.

As Josh fields phone calls, I wander into the street, ice cubes clinking against glass. Dogs bark in the distance. Mariachi music plays lightly a block or two away, and traffic rumbles from the nearby interstate — the sounds of lives moving on. The humidity dampens my skin and hair. I run through the large field owned by St. John's Church across the street, soles pounding against the earth, rigid and cracked from a drought that arrived long before we did. In the middle of that field, out of reach of streetlights with grass as stiff as hay beneath me, I down the last of my drink and chuck the pint glass into the air, waiting for the unbreaking thud of its return to earth. It falls and I crumble. The light of our front windows glows orange in the distance.

I can't put it together. Ours was the family that made people laugh and drew them in. Once, on a visit home, the doorbell rang and a friend of mine from third grade stood there, smiling at me.

"Hi?" I said.

"Oh, you're home! I'm sorry, I didn't know. I'll let you have your mom to yourself, but tell her I'll come back another time?"

"My mom?"

The friend gave me a confused little smile. "Yeah, she's the best.

But you know that. I come see her whenever I'm in town. I love how you can tell her anything and she understands. And jeez, is she funny or what?"

I watched as she drove off, wondering who my mother was in my absence. Party girl. Surrogate mother.

Just as common were friends of my brother's sticking their heads in the door, yelling, *Matt home?* Day, night, year after year. *Matt home? Matt home?* Any day with him felt like a party. We had real parties too — pool parties, graduation parties, birthday parties, surprise parties, random parties. What now? A funeral party?

Josh yells for me. I answer but can't stand. He follows my sound.

"Hey, you," he says. He holds me, his arms sticking to mine. "Come here."

"What time is it?"

"Maybe midnight. Maybe one."

My ankles tickle and sting. Tiny red specks move over my skin. "Fire ants," I say, pleased that we're witnessing together these creatures we were warned about. I feel all the tiny, stinging bites, but the pain is quaint compared to the rib-cracking pressure in my chest. At home, we rinse off my legs and watch the welts bubble up.

Around two or three that morning, our friend Neil knocks on the door. Neil and I met in a writing class in Montana and got into the same graduate program here in Texas. We told him he could crash with us after the long drive to Texas while he hunts for a place of his own. Neil has Richard Burton eyes and low expectations. He was raised in Idaho, the single defector in a large Mormon family. He reads the air the moment he steps inside — a barometer of grief.

"What's going on, guys?"

Josh and I stand still on the kitchen's green linoleum, the whir of the air conditioner making white noise. We look at each other to see who wants to tell Neil. We've spent hours on barstools in Montana with Neil. Neil has read nearly all of my "fiction" about my brother, every crazy story Matthew gave me fleshed out on the page in great detail, yet still falling flat. Neil, I think, will understand the enormity of this loss. Neil will be devastated. Josh nods and I say the words.

"Matthew shot himself in the head tonight."

"Shit, Mel." Neil runs a hand through his hair and exhales, shaking his head back and forth. "I'm fucking sorry," he says, "but I guess it's no big surprise."

The acceptance in Neil's ice-blue eyes unhinges me. If Matthew's death is no surprise to someone who didn't even know him firsthand, it should be no surprise to me. I should have done something. But you know what's as strange as the things we don't see coming? The things we see coming all along but don't believe will ever happen.

By the light of the next morning, we cruise ninety in the Honda all the way to the San Antonio airport. The highways here are vast: six lanes at the edge of town, up to ten as we navigate the flyovers, skirting the city to reach the airport. Someone booked a plane ticket to Georgia for me in the night, a night that ended in more vodka, dry heaves, and a blackout. We had no money for travel ourselves. No one to watch the dogs, even. Josh offered to hold down the homefront while I went to help my family claim my brother's body and deal with the wreckage he left behind. I woke hourly the whole night long, reckoning again and again with where I am (Texas) and what happened (suicide). At the departure drop-off, Josh holds my backpack while I slip my arms under the straps.

"You're on Delta," he says. "Ticket's paid for, just give them your

ID." He gives me a helpless look I'll see on the faces of so many in the days and weeks to come. "I'm sorry," he says. "Tell everyone I'm sorry."

I can't wrap my brain around this. *Sorry for what? You didn't do anything.* I nod. He is trying to be kind.

He pulls me in for a kiss and hug. "I love you," he says.

"I know." I head for the sliding doors, then remember. "Hey. I love you too."

The airline attendant does the math on my tears and bereavement fare and personally speed-walks me all the way to the gate, which is about to close. She gives my hand a squeeze, wishes me well.

Wishes. I have only one wish: Matthew alive. In the face of that impossibility, a second wish: to be nameless, anonymous, a helium balloon released. It sounds easy as slipping into the nearest bar. I'll have a drink, brush my hair in the bathroom, and come out a stranger. Solo. Singular.

But my body moves forward on autopilot. I board one plane, exit, board another. I can't stop crying. Face-wrenching tears. The woman next to me is brave enough to try to catch my eye. She hovers a hand over my forearm for a moment, then looks away. My head pounds — a sack of wet sand. It is all I can do to settle my eyes on the seat in front of me, a hand on each elbow as I rock myself back and forth the whole flight through.

The food tray hangs like a miniature movie screen on which I take inventory: the time Matthew stepped on a rusty nail at Mamaw's and ran home crying, the time he gave himself a mohawk with the dog clippers, the times we wore Star Wars T-shirts and swung on vines in Brown County, the time he snapped his wrist skateboarding, the time he broke his collarbone wrestling, times, full grown, he stood with me by the Christmas tree with beer in hand, and now this time. The time he put a gun to his head and died.

Time out. Time over. End times.

It is an ill-fitting piece that changes the whole puzzle, a piece I am left behind to justify.

On the ground in Atlanta, I walk through the tunnel that leads to the gate where my father, mother, and her siblings wait (Aunt Bonnie, Aunt Lisa, and Uncle Mark). I can't look at Mom, but I know she's there, being held up by her brother. Dad lifts his hands palm-up in a gesture equal parts surrender and confusion. I stumble in front of him, my legs dead, as people move around me without wavering, the way a river flows around a midstream boulder.

We board subway car 66. Between my new zip code (78666), the date of Matthew's death (8/6), and the subway number, it feels like the universe is playing a mean joke on me. The train is packed — no seats — so we hold on to poles as the car rumbles on, warm and dumb, pushing us through the underground into some future where I am an only child. Sobs wrench out of me erratically, and I feel like I'm underwater, trapped.

Before I know what's happening (time loses all order), we're buckled in a rented black SUV with tinted windows, the kind made to hide celebrities and criminals. It is a gas-guzzling giant of a car, taking us too quickly to a place I do and do not want to go. Uncle Mark drives, his head grazing the roof. The height gene missed me but hit my brother, a gift passed down through our maternal line, starting with our dead grandfather (the state trooper), gracing Uncle Mark, and hoisting Matthew above the six-foot mark as well. Matthew — our alien invader, a spontaneous flower in the abandoned lot of us.

First stop: a funeral parlor in Athens, Georgia, where his body lay in waiting.

August 6, 2000

Did thoughts or images run through his head in those thirty minutes while Randy held his hand and his heart still beat? Was his brain, mortally wounded, firing a final round of memories?

Like when he was three and four and five and spent hours in the backyard, his army men defeating platoons of black ants while he heard through the kitchen window his mother phone-talking with a sister — her voice his favorite sound in the universe.

From nowhere comes a flood of memory shrapnel: the scent of an old girlfriend (clove cigarettes and strawberry shampoo), his father's blue corduroy bell-bottoms, his sister screaming his name in a cornfield, the way the headliner in his first car hung down on his head after the glue dissolved, a dead hamster in a Ball jar, that old quilt his Mamaw made — the threads unraveling.

Is this a dream? Is he face-up in the grass again, back in Indiana? No.

He's lying spread-eagle on cheap linoleum with an oozing kind of relief around him — warm and wet — like an eardrum burst. He hears it then — the last sound in the world: his dog panting nearby.

Then he's somewhere else. Departed. Disembodied. The other side of the Quiet.

NINE

SUV

Georgia: August 7, 2000

*T*HE CARVED MORTUARY DOORS, painted red and gold, remind me of a midwestern Chinese restaurant. I push the giant handles until they open, overcome by the urge to demand my brother. Instinct trumps reason: Matthew doesn't belong here. *Give me give me give me.*

The others follow. Inside, darkness blinds us for a moment. Once our pupils dilate, we sit on a bench so large, I feel like Alice after her second bite of the mushroom. A potbellied man in a black suit whispers to my parents with practiced gentleness, *Matthew Stephenson . . . embalming but no preparation . . . follow me.*

The attendant leads Mom, Dad, and me down a hallway, his eyes averted. I want to stop our forward motion, say, *Wait. What even happened?*

No one has told us a thing other than Matthew shot himself dead. I don't know what it is that we are about to see. A body, yes. But will it look like my brother? Did he use a shotgun or a handgun? Did he put the barrel in his mouth or press it against his temple, or the forehead, behind the ear? Is his head intact or more like a blown-apart basketball? Because whatever we are about to see can't be undone.

The attendant leads us to another set of doors and reaches out to open them.

"Wait," I say. "I mean, does he even have a face?"

He looks at me, confused, as if my question is unusual, but he doesn't answer. Instead he waves us on, through a doorway.

First thing I notice is a clock marking the time: 4:47. I won't look at the white stretcher on the far side of the room. Chairs upholstered in silky black fabric embossed with dragons stand silent against the walls. The red carpet soaks up all sound. Same color as the red reading room in our hometown library, where Mom used to take Matthew and me for story time, the carpet pressing basket patterns into our knees as we sat mesmerized by the librarian's velvet voice.

Mom approaches the front of the room, mumbles something, and leaves, perfunctory and efficient — the period at the end of a sentence.

Dad stops ten feet from the stretcher. He breathes intermittently. *Breathe, breathe, breathe, stop. Inhale, exhale. Breathe, breathe, stop.* He's suspended, like an astronaut loose in space — unable to come closer, unable to leave.

Finally, I look at the body on the stretcher. My brother?

He has a face.

Years ago, on a high school backpacking trip, I ran naked into the clear blue waters of Lake Michigan in March and felt my chest collapse so completely, I barely made it out. It is this same kind of pressure that takes me down, a bone-crushing darkness that knocks my knees loose. I make my way to one of those dragon chairs and heave, head in hands, a hurricane of emotion I won't know again until five years later, when I birth my son — the feelings opposite but equal in intensity.

Matthew lies face-up, impossibly still, a starched white sheet over his comic-book arms.

I stay seated as each of my mother's siblings passes through. Bonnie makes it halfway across the room and leaves. Mark, the state trooper's son, dutifully nods at his nephew, his posture a brace over injury. Our Aunt Lisa crosses the distance in seconds. The only one to touch him, she reaches under the sheet for his hand and speaks to him in the same gravelly, chain-smoker voice that comforted us both through childhood. Then she leans down and kisses him goodbye. The backbone on her is something strong and wild as Matthew's beauty — a rare trait from the depths of our family tree.

They each pat my shoulder on their way out and remind me I can leave, that I don't have to do this.

But I do. After all, it is you, there. *You.*

I walk past our father, still lost in space, and come close enough to rest my hands on your stretcher. First thing I notice is how the center of your upper lip is anchored down — glued to your teeth. (You'd be enthralled with your own corpse, I know.) Your face is perfect aside from the absolute stillness. The way they bound your head in gauze reminds me of the years you wore a bandanna as a do-rag — a rare breed of Indiana vigilante. You have an icepack as a pillow, your head elevated like someone not dead but under a sleep curse in a fairy tale.

I imagine the entry and exit wounds buried beneath your gauze headdress, everything in between blasted clean through. Our father and mother will swear this is an accident. Aunt Lisa will back them up, say you were never anything less than happy, when the truth is you were never anything less than happy to see her.

The suited man returns and issues a reverse wave. It must be after five, but I can't go. We are minutes shy of a full twenty-four hours since you pulled the trigger. I am here, and your body, too.

If we could shift things into reverse — slam the universe into gear like a manual transmission with a bad clutch — the blood would go in, your brain reassemble, the bullet exit, and you'd stand up, embarrassed, apologizing forever.

"Let's go," our father says. He takes a step toward us, but my proximity to you makes him nervous.

"Another minute," I say, and he leaves the room, leaves me final witness.

How strange it is to see your body without you in it. I mean, I get it — your body was broken and you didn't know how to fix it, so you abandoned it like a beater in the breakdown lane.

I think about your tattoos, some hidden beneath the sheet, from the Lynyrd Skynyrd on your arm to those blue lightning bolts down yonder to the pterodactyl on your neck. Below your right ear, I spot something new. The words *Indiana Maiden* in a heavy-metal font. (If you'd put it anywhere else, I'd never have known.) It echoes the words newly inked on my own arm: *Made in Indiana* — a recent addition I was waiting to show you. I lean down to see it up close so years from now I can be certain of this, your unmistakable goodbye, hand-poked prison-style, just for me.

I never do touch you.

5:13. The great doors open again.

"Melissa," our father says.

My body turns away (hardest thing I ever do) while part of me stays forever in that room, caught in a trick of time between me and you.

TEN

Skyline Double Wide

Georgia: August 2000

*M*ONDAY AND THE SUN RISES in spite of us. By nine, the cloud cover burns off. It will be a hot one. The land- fill gate opens automatically, as if we're expected guests of the rich and famous.

Uncle Mark parks that death-dark SUV near the only struc- tures in sight — a pair of trailers. One serves as the administrative office for the Athens–Clarke County Landfill. The other sits back from the office. It's a doublewide trailer with brown shutters and white siding that reminds me of our first house by the cemetery. It is Matthew's trailer. Or it was.

The landscape resembles a model of Mars's surface I con- structed out of papier-mâché in fifth grade: brown hills of dirt and debris, void of green. Matthew must have felt at ease here for the same reason he loved apocalyptic movies like *Red Dawn* and *Mad Max:* He could relax around such destruction, become king of the castoffs, prince of the misfits. The sick, sweet smell of earth and garbage intensifies under full sun. Did he carry traces of that scent with him when he hit the town, hair slicked back with Royal

Crown, donning a vintage button-down. Did he even notice the stench anymore, or had decay become part of him?

A man near Matthew's age introduces himself as Greg and unlocks the trailer door. His eyes look like ours: red and swollen with grief. Dad climbs the two steps to the door and cracks it slowly, glancing back to gauge if we're ready. (We are not.) He pushes the door and lets it swing open on its own before stepping inside. No one tells us if the place has been cleaned. (No one tells us anything.) I follow in my father's footsteps. (It has.)

The trailer is a late-eighties Skyline, a model with a pitched roof that most consider a step up from the flat-roofed models of the sixties and seventies. The main room is an open kitchen/living space larger than any house I've lived in as an adult. It inspires the same kind of awe that settled over me every time Matthew let me into his basement bedroom, which happened annually, at best. Once the bedroom became mine? No more magic. Just me.

Everything is white — walls, floors, countertops. The vaulted ceilings feel like church overhead, and silence settles over us as we register what remains. Salvaged easy chairs sit in the corner, near the stereo and record collection. Taped to the fridge is a recent Polaroid of Matthew wearing only his workboots. He sits in the easy chair, nude and laughing, while his cattle dog humps his leg. He'd spent the past few years getting tattoos at breakneck speed and ramping up his bizarre circus acts, like the leg-humping, and elaborate Halloween costumes worn sometimes on Halloween, sometimes on a Wednesday in February.

Greg stands behind the breakfast bar with his hands in pockets and feet apart, braced. He glances out the kitchen window, toward the road and the office trailer. I try to picture Matthew in this room, but he seems too big for it somehow, despite the vaulted ceilings.

"He did it in the kitchen?" Dad's voice is careful and low.

"Yes, sir. About where I'm standing." Greg raises a hand to cover his trembling chin — a strained levee. He is about Dad's size — just under six feet, slight build, overgrown brown hair, a bit of a Gram Parsons.

Dad's eyes ricochet from the window to Greg to the ceiling. He lifts his hand and starts to ask a question, but my mother interrupts.

"It's so clean in here —" she says, a sob cutting her sentence short.

"Yes, ma'am. I stayed up all night, cleaned everything." Greg steps aside and regards the spot where Matthew's body must have fallen. "I cleaned the floors a few times, moved the stove, and then —"

That is not what she meant. She meant *clean* as in *tidy,* as in *everything in this trailer has a place,* that her son carried her OCD gene after all. The silver faucet shines. Ashtrays stand empty. Albums arranged by the shades of their spines.

Not *clean* as in *scrubbed free of her son's blood.*

"I'm sorry," Greg says.

A man in uniform and mirrored sunglasses knocks as he walks in, introduces himself, and asks for the deceased's parents. My folks step forward and shake hands with him. He is the sheriff, here to walk us through the logistics of death. Round but tall, he speaks with a drawl that feels like fresh paint over a rust spot. He greets us, then excuses himself for a moment to verify the crime scene report. He returns with two shotguns, one short, one long.

"Bad boy," he says. "Playing with loaded weapons."

Playing. He thinks my brother was *playing?*

"But he sawed this one off within a millimeter of legal. Boy knew his stuff."

He talks about Matthew like he's a juvenile delinquent. Another piece of trash in this landfill. He unloads the guns, tossing one of the shells in the air and catching it before putting it in his pocket.

"He stood right here, probably looking out the window," he says, hooking thumbs in belt loops as he speaks. "He used the Glock, which is why the exit wound wasn't too big. Nice and clean, really. Good thing he didn't use the shotgun."

"Where was the exit wound again?" Dad says.

"Right side."

"Then he would have used his left hand. Why would he use his left hand?"

The sheriff shrugs as if the point is moot. "It will take a couple weeks for his blood alcohol report to come back, but it appears he was drunk, so maybe that's why."

We pause to consider this detail.

"It was an accident," Aunt Lisa says, a possibility watered with hope.

"Well, no. Let's see, I got it wrong." The sheriff clears his throat. "Left-side exit wound. He used his right hand. See the bullet hole in the ceiling? Right hand, looking out the kitchen window, the impact spun him a bit, bullet exited to the left, and he fell right here. Done."

I can't stop making a mental list of the sheriff's word choices: *Nice, clean, good,* and *done.*

Outside, a car door slams, and Randy comes up the stairs — one of Matthew's best friends. Also from Indiana. The last person to see him alive.

Randy scans our faces and shuts his eyes. He runs a hand over his own face as if to reset, then addresses us all. "I got something for you guys."

He yells for Early Times, Matthew's overweight cattle dog, who barrels through the open door. A black spot over the left eye punctuates Early's salt-and-pepper body. The dog does his own walk-through to be sure: No Matthew.

With his shark smile on and his ears slicked back, Early returns to the main room, sniffs us one by one, then sits at my feet, looks me straight in the face. For the next few years I will not so much as go to the bathroom alone.

"That your dog?" the sheriff says to me.

"No. Well. Maybe now."

We break the silence to pet Early and greet Randy. The sheriff excuses himself. Mom and Aunt Lisa light cigarettes and crack sodas from the fridge. Inside they find a cafeteria tray half filled with Dixie cups of Jell-O shots. While they take long drags of their Virginia Slims, Dad steps into the lull.

"So you were with him," he says to Randy.

Randy's breath quivers on the uptake. "Yes, sir."

Consider this: Your brother did not die but (your mother says) went to live on a farm in the country where he had plenty of room to roam.

Randy confirms what we all thought — Matthew had been sober mostly, going to AA meetings and trying hard to stick with it. But last week, the week after his twenty-ninth birthday, he started in again. He spent nights downtown so drunk he could barely walk. He kept his new girlfriend at arm's length, the one he'd described to me on the phone last spring, saying she "looks like a midget only real pretty." Corey, his estranged wife who'd moved back to L.A., had been calling, leaving messages, threatening a visit.

Matthew drank harder.

He bragged about seducing one woman in the cereal aisle at his local grocery by putting a hand on the small of her back and asking if she'd like to play Jack and Diane, after the John Cougar Mellencamp song. (She would.) Another girl reported seeing him drunk on a bench downtown the last Saturday of his life. She watched him fall off, crawl back up, fall off again, and doze. *I feel terrible,* she told us later. *I loved Matt, but I didn't want to get involved.*

Sunday morning he woke up alive, made a tray of Jell-O shots, and called his friends over one at a time. The ones who didn't answer, he crank called, assuming random accents and claiming to have fucked their girlfriends. That's how he got Randy out to the trailer — by harassing him in deepening degrees of drunkenness until he showed.

They talked for a while, as much as my brother could talk after downing shots all day long. Near the end, Matthew tried to provoke Randy into punching him. He wanted his own front teeth knocked out, imagining his face restored to those years between his baby teeth getting pulled and his permanent teeth erupting, those years when our Mamaw cut the corn off the cob for him and his only worries involved keeping track of his army men and figuring out how to make his own nunchucks.

"I talked him into sleeping it off," Randy says. "I put him to bed like he was a kid. He was out of it, eyes closed. I thought he was asleep. I drove down to the gate and realized Matt'd catch hell from management in the morning if they found it unlocked, so I drove back to the trailer to get the key. I was gone five minutes, tops." Randy looks at us, opens his mouth to say something, but finds no words.

Five minutes.

When he walked into the trailer, he noticed Matthew's feet sticking out from behind the breakfast bar. He rounded the corner, part of him knowing already.

"I saw his head, all that blood, and I thought, *Shit, Matt, you really fucked up this time.*" Randy's voice breaks. He inhales and exhales deeply for a half-minute, like a diver about to go under. A decade or so from now, he will tattoo Matthew's face on his left thigh along with the words *Know Regrets,* but even that won't mend what's busted in him.

"There was a sawed-off shotgun on the counter, but the Glock was on the floor next to him. I put the shotgun in his bedroom because I didn't want him to get in trouble. Stupid, I know, but I couldn't think. Then I called the cops and sat with him. He still had a heartbeat. For about a half-hour, his heart kept going. I could feel it, so I just sat with him and held his hand and told him it was going to be okay, but the way his eyes were open . . . I knew it was bad."

Randy's chest deflates as he exhales.

Nothing moves in the trailer other than our breathing.

He was here and now gone.

After a few long minutes, my family begins talking again, asking unanswerable questions, building conspiracy theories to explain away the gray. No matter what narrative they spin, the algebra comes out the same. *He lived and now doesn't. Was and isn't. Here and gone.*

Time seems impossible.

I walk through the doublewide, void of color aside from the chairs and albums and books, and I realize how little I know about my brother's life. How little I know my brother. He was my favorite person — parts of him so close I could barely distinguish him from myself. But other traits seem to belong to a stranger, like the two loaded shotguns, the Glock, and a book by his bedside: *Redneck Manifesto.* I remember him talking about the author, Jim Goad, with the reverence our father reserved for Carl Jung. Goad's central thesis, as far as I could tell from what Matthew told me and the few pages I scan, is that *white trash* is the only socially acceptable racial slur, making poor white men the last public punching bags.

I remember nodding as Matthew told me about Goad during a recent visit. I waited for him to explain why on earth he was reading this book and telling me about it. I blushed when I understood

Matthew saw himself as "white trash," or at least he thought others did. Here was my Midas, walking through life feeling like a leper — a notion so heart-rending that I put it to bed in the darkest, quietest part of my brain with the hope, perhaps, that it would die there.

Some divide beyond physical distance had opened between Matthew and me when we left home. I'd spent four years at Interlochen living with people from all over the world. Another student, a few years ahead of me, was a prince from Ghana and a hell of a writer and drummer. There was Nate from Pakistan whose full name I loved to hear but could never pronounce. Kiku from Hawaii. Rioso from Japan. Karen from Detroit, who taught me that black folks' hair required different handling than white folks' hair. There were local students — the kids of teachers — whose backwoods style started a Red Wing boot trend. There were gay kids, cross-dressing kids, and though we never used a name for it back then, certainly transgender kids.

All the while, Matthew had stayed in Indiana, nurturing the anger of a white boy who had been raised like a prince only to discover himself part toad and the story of his unlimited potential a hoax. In its place he found a multiple-choice test for the future. Become

a) a college kid
b) a manual laborer
c) a junkie
d) all of the above
e) other

He tried like hell to choose *other.* When that option kept failing, Jim Goad gave him permission to turn his shame into blame. The target? A faceless thing called Society, which must have felt liberating. The problem was *them,* not *him.*

If he'd known the people I had known in my teen years, I wondered, would he have grown up different? Would that thing in him that turned so brittle that it broke have stayed open and pliant?

I continue through the rooms with Early Times at my heels, remembering a disturbing story Matthew told about Early that I laughed at, so ingrained was my habit of compliance. He tormented his girlfriend with a threat to take Early to a whorehouse for a blowjob before getting him neutered. This was performance, I knew. Once he finished telling the story (in front of the girlfriend and our family), he leaned over to me and said, *Write that down, Missy. All you have to do is write that shit down.*

It was a side of my brother that always felt like a caricature — part stranger, part blue-collar song-and-dance man.

He once tried to tell me something about this dark part of him, late one night while we were both visiting Indiana over the holidays with one of Mom's five trees blinking behind us. He said, *I don't get it, Missy. I can be the life of the party like Mom, then I can be a total stick-in-the-mud like Dad. I can't just change my mind. I can't control it. And sometimes? I just want to bash my own face in. It's a craving, like being hungry.* What I didn't have the words to tell him, or even the wisdom to know, is that this was a thing someone could diagnose, and treat. If he'd made it that far.

Consider this: Your brother did not die but went off to war and came back a thrice-decorated hero with eyes full of dead children.

I shove mementos of the brother I did know in my backpack the way I once pocketed cassette tapes and books from his bedroom on the sly. I sort through his collection of concert shirts, setting aside a signed Misfits tee he wore for most of his fifteenth summer. I find a stack of patches cut from work shirts he likely found at the dump: Ford, Skeeter, Raymond, Couey Logging (because it was close to Corey?), and Henderson Trucking (saved for my husband,

I'm sure). It feels like I've been granted VIP access to the most personal kind of museum.

Matthew always collected things, hoarded them. At age five, he already had a collection of collections: GI Joes, ninja weapons, wrestling cards, Star Wars figures, and gold coins that sparkled like a sky full of stars in the slots of the blue plastic pages. I remember us as kids, bath-damp in our pajamas, huddled around his precious coin collection as if the glow of the gold were a bonfire. I wore my softest Holly Hobby nightgown — the one with ruffles and bluebonnets. Matthew was a superhero. Belly-down on shag carpet, I angled for a view, but Matthew wouldn't have it. He took those heavy metal pages and scooted away, looking back for a moment to punch fist into open palm — a warning. The second time I sidled up, he whispered a threat. We could spend whole evenings like that: me inching toward him while he enforced a radius of lonesome around me the length of a full-grown man. Not a thing in that house bought me a glimpse of those dead presidents, their value skyrocketing under the weight of my desire.

In another dresser drawer I find a notebook of his poems and take it. I take the Lucinda Williams album from the CD player, and a mix tape I once made him from the cassette deck — likely the last music he heard.

I take the letter from one of his childhood idols: Lemmy, the frontman for the band Motörhead. Matthew's wife, Corey, had been the fire-breathing bass player for a southern metal band called Nashville Pussy. They had opened for part of Motörhead's tour. I'd heard from our dad in the past year that Matthew thought Corey had slept with Lemmy, and that's why Matthew left her and came back to Athens. The letter is handwritten and three pages long, sealed in a Ziploc baggie like a piece of evidence. It reads like something a sixth-grader might compose in the middle of the night, so unclear that I can't tell if it's an apology or a denial. I picture Matthew, torn been between anger and reverence, as he read and reread that letter, alone in this trailer in Georgia.

In the bedroom I empty a metal ashtray that first belonged to our folks and add it to my pile.

The trailer continues to grow on me. It is, after all, the original tiny home on wheels. With a trailer you can set down roots and pack up shop in a pinch, hit the road, and plant yourself again. I wonder if he thought of those wheels below him as he slept. Near the foot of his bed — kicked off in the heat of the night, I imagine — a navy and white star quilt our Mamaw made him rests in a pile. I own the sister quilt (a red star). I take his, too.

"Missy," Dad calls from the living room.

He hasn't called me by my nickname in years. It sounds important. A note? He's kneeling near the easy chair, in front of the shelves of books and records. He's pulled out a whole stack of papers in plastic bags.

"This is all yours," he says. His voice catches so that it takes a few breaths for him to get out the next words. "Looks like everything you ever wrote."

I sit down and inspect the pile. There's the chapbook I handmade at Interlochen, my two-hundred-page thesis, a half-dozen short stories, and pages of stray poems. My handwritten letters, too. Every single thing I'd written, in chronological order, curated.

I don't have to wonder anymore. I am holding the proof, the answer to that long-ago Interlochen study partner's question: My brother and I *are* close. At least, we were.

I take my writing. I take his journals, filled with poems in his angular script. I take a stack of pictures without sifting through them. I take some books I find on his shelf: three novels I sent him in spring when he spent a month in a prison with his coworker Victor as part of the job training needed to supervise the criminals bused in to work at the landfill. I open each book to read my inscriptions (the first, black pen on dark green paper — only half wanting to be found). The pages are dog-eared, the spines broken. It means everything to me that he read them, maybe finding relief from loneliness in those paragraphs the way I always have, always will. I wrap my loot in the star quilt and step outside, finished.

Consider this: Your brother did not die but went to rehab, became a lifelong member of AA, and spent the rest of his life trying to save everyone (especially you).

We spend two days in Athens disassembling my brother's life. Time moves forward, minutes ticking by like insults. Friends of Matthew's tell stories about his final months, how he spent a lot of time shooting dead things at the dump. This is the part of him that picked fights he never planned to win, the part of him that drank all the drinks, the part of him that said *you stupid fucking redneck* while he tried to pull out his own front teeth with pliers, in a blackout. It's the part of him that didn't see the privilege of his gender and skin color because when a door opened for him — a door to art school or college or even the high school wrestling club — he couldn't muster the self-esteem to make an entrance.

We sign papers, pay bills, pack up for donation the things no one will take, and collect his personal items from the police department (chain wallet, driver's license, a twenty-spot). Between errands, we visit his two favorite restaurants, where all we can do is drink. Dad's blood sugar goes low one evening and he disappears in a nearby park for hours, talking in turns to the ground and sky.

The second night, Mom and I don't even try to crawl into the hotel bed. Instead, we drink all night on a grassy knoll. I read poetry aloud, insisting each line is an answer. A stranger rolls out of a frat party around four in the morning and chats us up.

I tell him to fuck himself.

Mom gives him Matthew's twenty-spot and tells him to get a cab home as the night sky bleeds into a southern dawn.

That final morning in Georgia, I try to put my contacts in so I can wear sunglasses on the drive back to Texas. (I will not be flying.) My eyes burn, the contacts two spots of fire. I stare into the hotel mirror, half blind. Mom stares back from behind me, her face ripe with worry.

"Oh, honey," she says, "your eyes."

I look down at the vanity and notice I've used Visine instead of saline solution.

"It's going to be okay," Mom says, wrapping her arms around me.

"No," I say. "I'm pretty sure these are fucked." I wiggle out of her embrace, rip the contacts from my eyes, and fling them against the mirror, where they cling — two tiny wrinkles in our reflection.

Mom steps back.

I open my mouth but don't say what I know: The world will never look the same again.

For the first time in my life, I have no desire to travel. I don't want to go forward, only back to the Skyline to tuck my wheels up under my skirt (like her) and think my way back to a world where my brother will one day be an uncle, and some child might call me *aunt*. Back to a story where he lives and loves me.

Instead, my family drops me at the dump on their way to the airport. In between the drinks, breakdowns, and blackouts of the past two days, it has been decided that I will take Early Times (the dog everyone regards the way they do performance art — remarkable but not lovable). The only way to get the dog named after a cheap brand of whiskey back to Texas is to drive my brother's new favorite thing: a cherry-red 1979 Ford F-150.

Part 3

ELEVEN

The Vanagon

On the Road: 1994–98

*T*HERE'S SOMETHING I NEED to tell you, but I can't because there are no words. No words to describe inhabiting a body vacated by drive. No words for how I am no longer *little sister* or *wife* or *she,* but a wound in a human costume. No words for the nothing I feel about Matthew's big red Ford, other than dumbstruck by how frivolous it now seems that I ever loved cars at all.

Without Matthew, I'm beyond fear and time and lonely. His absence leaches into my bones, which become tuning forks for the wind. The "real" world feels like a television show on mute, under water, infecting my head with a permanent white noise. A sound like the ocean inside a seashell. The sound of quiet, amplified, waves of stillness vibrating around you. It is the sound of a haunting, and it takes me all the days in Georgia to realize that it is now the inescapable sound of me.

Vodka cranberries don't dull the sound. Closing my eyes doesn't turn it down. Sobs arrive like seizures, leaving me so still afterward that my heartbeat slows between breaths. The only thing that distracts from this un-sound, this sonic absence, is following my brain where it runs — miles and years back — to glimpses of Matthew I pushed away so I could believe in the story of our family, the story we all wanted to be true. Now the evidence rears its head, demanding to be counted, his death lurking between frames.

How did he get so lost? And how had I gotten so lost that I hadn't seen it coming? Or did I? Did we?

One day we were alive in a Squareback, singing songs of our own creation. Another day we were swimming in our new in-ground pool under a hot July sky. Another we were opening presents on Christmas, bedhead until noon, mimosas all around.

The stories that return to me now are the ones between these greeting-card memories. They are the glitches we'd tried to erase because they didn't fit. Like the time Dad sideswiped a tree with the Volaré, only weeks off the lot. We all stared down at the dent the size of half a basketball and agreed: *It'll buff right out.*

Like the time we glossed over Matthew's near death in a cornfield outside of Vincennes, or normalized his doomed marriage, or ignored his absence at my wedding, or that last time we saw him — in the final days of 1999. He'd returned to Indiana to try to stay alive, and all we knew how to offer, without words, was that same old message, flat as a worn-out tire: *It'll all buff out.*

The Vincennes Incident lives in my brain like it's my own experience. I can't even recall how the story came to me, through Dad or Mom or Matthew or his girlfriend Jenny Irene. It goes like this: Matthew mumbles some defiant shit to a pack of university basketball players on a drunk Saturday night. They posture. He holds his ground, Jenny pulling his arm, saying *let's go let's go just let it go.* He tells her to go home, and says, low but clear, the thing that makes the bartender tell them to take it outside, where he finds not a fair fight but a battle against the whole team. The lead pipe breaking Jenny's nose and teeth when she tries to intervene sends him into a full-on rage. He takes a hit to the skull, then nothing until the heavy throb of his head on damp soil wakes him up in the middle of a cornfield. They must have dumped him there to die, or thought him dead already. But he rises, slowly, with the sun, not tall enough to see above the stalks, and too injured to jump. He does the thing Dad and Mamaw said to do if you ever get lost in a cornfield: pick one row and follow it out. Otherwise you could walk and weave forever, circling back, getting nowhere. Soon he finds the road, where no one will stop because of the blood, and walks himself into town, back home, to Jenny, who holds him and cries while he says, *it's okay, baby, it's okay.*

It happened the summer of '94. Matthew showed up at our folks' house for a few days soon after with his face busted but spirits intact. Our parents were worried and angry. They wanted to call the cops, press charges, and send Matthew to the doctor. They wanted answers, but Matthew had no interest. The important thing, he wanted us to know, is that he was okay.

It was the last summer the two of us would spend any real chunk of time in Indiana. I'd come home after working at Interlochen, where I'd sold the Saab to Delp. Dad had found my next new-to-me car. Or van, rather: a brown 1984 Volkswagen Vanagon. The love was deep and instant, and Matthew let me give him a little tour before we both left town again. I showed him the curtains I'd sewn on Mom's machine and the track I'd rigged for them using rope. Dad had built a platform in back so the seat could fold out into a queen-size bed. As I talked, a darkness settled over my brother's bruised face. He shot me a look I hadn't seen in a long while, the look he gave me often in the days when he called me the Princess, after the Shirley Temple film by the same name.

"Mom and Dad bought you this?" he said.

"We went halvsies," I answered, though I realized as I spoke that those words weren't quite true. This time I'd only contributed the money from the sale of the Saab, and my parents covered the other two thirds of the cost.

Matthew nodded, arms crossed.

"They'll help you if you want a car."

"I don't want a car."

"What do you want?" I blushed as soon as I asked this. I hadn't meant to become another person questioning him, like our parents. My own wants were so large and overwhelming that I truly wondered about his.

"Nothing," Matthew said. "I don't want nothing." He did that thing again where he dumbed down his speech on purpose. Then he put on a big fake grin and made small talk before he went his way and I went mine.

Consider this: The year Matthew was born, Dad brought home a Pinto instead of a Fiat, and the family enjoyed fifteen minutes of fame, aflame on the nightly news after a rear-end collision made the gas tank explode — all three of them extinguished before you were born.

Back in Montana, my van travels continued, uninhibited by my class schedule. I drove to San Francisco for a Grateful Dead show once, the van hanging in for twenty hours straight at speeds over eighty while I split driving shifts with friends, half of us asleep on the bed in back as the desert passed by, dark and barren. On my twenty-first birthday, I headed into the Canadian Rockies with Vanessa, my new best friend. We hunted down one of her childhood friends from New York City who had run away. By some miracle, we found her in a shack full of hippies at the base of a mountain known for its natural hot springs. I let Vanessa drive for a stretch on the way back, telling her to wake me at a certain gas station before we reached the border. I woke to her yelling *fuck fuck fuck* as she coasted into customs.

They pulled us over, pulled us out, and sequestered us in individual search rooms. When the customs agent asked me to empty my pockets, I looked down at the series of flaps, zippers, and pockets within pockets on my Liberty overalls and laughed (a bad move). *Which one?* I asked. My search came up clean but they found .05 ounces of marijuana in a film canister in the van — a birthday gift from my third college boyfriend, a kind-eyed guy with dreadlocks from Billings. I accepted the charges and drove us home.

Over the next year, I worked a restaurant job and went to school part time so that I could earn in-state tuition, which would save my folks some cash. I met Josh and, in the first days of 1996, drove us from Montana to Indiana through a record-breaking blizzard. We sometimes couldn't see the road. I had my first dog by then, who rode in an olive-green easy chair I'd found near a dumpster. I'd unscrewed the legs so the chair sat flat on the van floor, making a perfect raised bed for the dog. The van got so cold on that adventure that my accelerator foot went numb in my wool-lined boots even with the heat on full blast. The dog drooled as we drove on, her saliva freezing into a stalagmite.

We made the trip over the great prairies to the Midwest once or twice a year in that van. She ran and ran and ran.

Josh borrowed her regularly once he realized how the open cargo space made loading up his band equipment easy. The floor of the van sat lower than a trunk or truck bed — heaven for a musician's back. Josh had never owned a car — an odd thing for a kid from the West, but he was a city kid in Montana terms. His parents had divorced when he was eight, and his mom died suddenly when he was eighteen. His estranged father lived in the country with his new family, and his stepdad quickly remarried after his mother's death. Josh was a bit of an orphan, and smart enough to know he could walk from class to the bars and back. He wouldn't have driven at all if not for my van. As little as I knew about the mechanics of cars, he knew less. If a check engine light went off, I pulled over immediately while he'd drive on, immune, his brain tuned to melodies and lyrics.

In the spring of '97, Josh and I drove the van to Las Vegas for my cousin Chad's wedding. My mother and her siblings had taken up gambling and vacationing in the nineties. The eighties had been good to them, and they could now afford Caribbean cruises and Vegas trips. Chad, Aunt Bonnie's only child, was born six months before Matthew. A quiet, grounded, kindhearted person, he grew up with my brother, the two of them spending long days in the woods during summer weeks at Betty's house in Brown County.

My folks bought Matthew a plane ticket from Atlanta to Vegas for the wedding. My brother had been on an airplane only once or twice before then. From the moment Josh and I parked the Vanagon at the Flamingo Hilton and found my aunts, uncles, and cousins poolside, conversation revolved around the odds of Matthew showing up.

Did he have a ride to the airport? Had he called home recently? Did he have a phone? Had anyone heard?

Since he'd moved to Georgia, each Christmas became a cliff-hanger: Would Matthew show? He always did, never on time, but that did nothing to diminish our joy and relief when he walked through the door. He was a kind of celebrity in our family, with a special ability to cause more happiness and concern than any other one of us.

My parents were off getting room keys and Josh had just handed me a giant drink with fruit in it when I saw him coming from yards away. He wore mirrored sunglasses, a snug-fitting Hawaiian shirt, cutoffs, and his trademark Converse high-tops. He carried only a black backpack, small enough for a kid. After everyone hugged him, I offered him the lounge chair next to mine. I was in my swimsuit already.

"Where's your suitcase?" I said.

"Right here." He unzipped the Jansport to show me what he'd packed, proud of how little he needed: one apple, underwear, a toothbrush, plus the dog-eared paperback *And I Don't Want to Live This Life* — a book about Nancy Spungen, girlfriend of Sid Vicious, who was found stabbed to death in their room at the Chelsea Hotel in 1978. It was one of Matthew's favorite love stories.

"Good book," I said. We could always talk books and music. I was kind of thrilled that out of all our family, Matthew chose to sit by me.

A security guard approached and demanded Matthew's room key. Matthew didn't have one, and the guard wouldn't accept mine even though we were staying in the same room with two queen beds.

"Every guest needs a key," the guard said. "Or they have to leave the premises."

"Our parents are getting his now," I said.

The guard called for backup on his walkie-talkie, and a crowd began to form. He launched one question after another, talking over Matthew's answers: *Where's your swimsuit?*

Didn't bring one.

Where do you live?

Georgia.

Why are you here?

A wedding.

Where's your luggage?

Here.

Open it up.

"You don't have to —" our Aunt Lisa said. I could tell she was scared about what might be inside.

Matthew smiled a thank-you to her and unzipped his backpack. The slim contents only irritated the guard, who returned to questions about the room key.

It finally sank in that he'd profiled Matthew as a bit of street trash washed up at their pool for some free casino drinks, a drug deal, or worse. Discovering he was attached to our family didn't help. They wanted him out.

Aunt Lisa removed her Amber Vision shades and stepped between the guard and Matthew.

"This," she said, "is discrimination. You, of all people, should know something about that." She pointed to his nametag — Carl. We all knew she was talking about his light brown skin and kinky hair. He was clearly biracial, or "mixed" as they'd say back home.

"I'm an office-holding Republican — clerk of Boone County, Indiana — and, Carl, the Flamingo Hilton CEO is going to hear about this incident."

"It's okay," Matthew said. "He's just doing his job." He smiled, calm in his role as suspect.

Soon my folks arrived with the room keys and cleared things up.

"That was so wrong," I said. "I'm sorry."

Matthew closed his eyes in the sun, holding the daiquiri Mom brought him and looking a bit like Hunter S. Thompson.

"That?" he said. "Shit. He didn't even cuff me."

Our father had a way of being in the world similar to Matthew. He'd grown up poor, quiet, good-looking, more interested in Kerouac and Kesey than sports or church. Good with the ladies. His aloof demeanor got his nose broken nine times in high school. For Matthew, the Vegas incident was a chance for his family to witness his persecution.

"Why not swim?" I said. "It's hot."

While I enjoyed the trappings of the fine life, Vegas held all the appeal of a shopping mall to me. Everything a shiny, plastic, hollow bauble. A place without choice or consequence.

"I got a new tattoo I can't get wet," Matthew said. "On my meat. Two lightning bolts. Don't tell Mom."

I'd always hated that word my family used for male genitalia: *meat*. So coarse. It made me cringe.

This news was his version of an ace up the sleeve, I guess. And I didn't tell Mom. I knew he'd do that himself in his own good time.

In the summer of '97, I got the wild idea to spend a couple months hiking a section of the Appalachian Trail. It would be my last summer before college graduation, and Grandma Betty had set aside several hundred dollars for each grandchild to take a trip. Our cousin Chad had gone to Guam and for reasons I can't recall. I was the second grandchild to propose a trip, and she granted me the funds.

While I loved driving above and beyond most anything else, some natural shift was happening. Josh drank a lot. Mom drank a lot. Matthew was a mess of booze and tattoos and bizarre stories my family treated like jokes. All the while diabetes continued erasing my father. Not long before my Appalachian Trail idea hit, a pack of generic cigarettes and a fast food fish sandwich downed on a long road trip inspired me to become a vegetarian, quit smoking again, and start running (all at the same time). My kin, ill versed in self-care, offered wary support.

I was already too serious for my family, too driven, "a stick-in-the-mud" as my brother had put it. Now here I was, going off-script in pursuit of health and happiness.

Josh and I drove the van from Montana to Georgia, where I would start my walk in the woods at the southernmost trailhead in Springer Mountain, only an hour or so from where Matthew lived in Athens. We visited him for a couple days. I don't recall much from that time other than the bars we went to, my brother's stunned reverence over my latest adventure, and his new girlfriend, Krista with the red pigtails, whom we all hoped he might marry.

"Hell, Missy," he said. "You're going to walk across the damn country on purpose and I don't walk farther than my mailbox unless I have to." He had color in his cheeks and a healthy bit of weight to him. (Like my father and me, he ran on the slim side, forgetting to eat when life got chaotic.)

In a single photo from the Athens leg of that trip, Josh and Matthew stand beside each other with the Vanagon in the background. Her sliding door is open, showing off the curtains, the easy chair, the bed in back. Matthew wears a fat tie from the seventies and a short-sleeve button-down. (He and Krista were on their way to a wedding, and she'd found that tie for him.) His tattooed knuckles wrap around the spine of a book Krista gave him: *Men Are from Mars, Women Are from Venus,* which he carried around as a catalyst for jokes more than anything. Josh sports horn-rims and a Unabomber beard. Wild garlic blooms in the yard behind them.

The next morning, Josh dropped me at the trailhead with my pack and I tried not to think about him driving my van all the way back to Montana.

I walked for two months straight, through magnolia blooms and torrential rains and mountains haunted by feral pigs. I walked through stress fractures, lost toenails, and bruised hipbones. Then I walked some more, finishing up somewhere in Virginia.

Back home after my return, Josh had put on a layer of weight that would remain for the length of our marriage, and the van started to fill with blue smoke every now and then. The oil light on the dash lit up. I added a quart and kept driving. I checked the coolant and added water instead of antifreeze because the German engineers had put a wave icon and the word *water* on the tank. Clouds of blue smoke erupted from the Vanagon's hindquarters, as regular as Old Faithful. I'd add another quart and keep on going. After few months of this, a cop pulled me over to point out the trail of smoke I'd left on the interstate.

"Blue means engine trouble," he said. I'd never before had a car with engine trouble. I always sold them before I had to deal with that. He let me off with a warning and told me to see a mechanic. I did.

Blown head gasket. Cylinder wear. Partial rebuild.

"But I kept putting oil in when the light went off," I told the mechanic, as if I could erase the damage with reason.

"The oil light?"

"Yeah, on the dash."

"That's not an oil level light, honey. That's oil pressure. You see that light go off and you'd better cut the engine right away. Low oil pressure means your engine is failing. It's got nothing to do with how much oil is in the engine. Hell, I'm surprised you didn't blow the main seal adding all that oil."

He let me go before my chin tremble gave way to tears of shame. The kind that belonged to a child, not a road warrior. Not me.

Dad bailed me out on the rebuild. I went two months in the middle of winter with no vehicle. Josh and I would walk to the grocery store, him with his army duffle and me wearing my Appalachian Trail pack. We'd load up all the dog food, potatoes, and bread we could carry and walk the mile and a half home.

I drove the van more gently when she came back, heeded all warning lights, and only filled the oil after consulting the dipstick. Still, I had no business driving that vehicle. Matthew had been right — she was more than I deserved.

TWELVE

The Planes

Georgia: February 1999

*T*O *GET ANYWHERE FROM MISSOULA*, you have to take two planes. The first is always a small plane (the kind with two seats on each side of the aisle), which delivers you to one of the nearby hubs: Minneapolis, Salt Lake, sometimes Denver. The second plane is, almost always, a Boeing 737, larger, with three seats on each side. It was on the second flight, the 737, in February of 1999 that Josh asked me to page the flight attendant and request an ice pick so he could stab himself in the eardrum to relieve the pressure.

His drama surprised me. I was usually the sensitive, moody one, and he played the good-natured steady. We were more than three years into our relationship by then, and I had begun to realize that my mate did not travel well.

My parents had bought us the plane tickets so we could fly to Indiana and drive with them down to Athens for Matthew's wedding. Only months ago, he'd fallen in love with Corey Parks — the woman we knew only as the bass player for Nashville Pussy. Just before Christmas he announced that they would marry.

I wouldn't have missed my brother's wedding if I'd had to walk there — a wedding that turned out to be a grand act of theater involving some of our family's most brazen enabling, if it was anything at all.

In Athens, we packed into my parents' hotel suite, waiting for Matthew and Corey to show up. My folks had met her for the first time the month before, but I had not yet had the pleasure.

Matthew knocked, and Mom opened up.

Corey stood long and lean as a rock 'n' roll scarecrow. She neared six-five with her boots on — all limbs and eyeliner — part Amazon woman and part Rod Stewart. Tattoos marked her from neck to knuckle, same as my brother. From the gap between the top of her leather hip-huggers and the bottom of her skintight tank-top, giant eagle wings rose up, eclipsing her womb. Matthew had told me over the phone that they'd gotten matching Lynyrd Skynyrd tattoos on their forearms. I noticed them immediately: a pair of red hearts with lettered banners. Relationship birthmarks.

She ducked through the doorway, hugged my mother, and moved on to me. She hooked her arms under mine, pulling my head uncomfortably into her sternum. She smelled like cigarettes, makeup, and some sort of chemical (perhaps the Coleman lamp fluid she drank and regurgitated on stage to breathe fire).

She gave me a solid five minutes of her attention, feeling obligated, perhaps, to make nice with her beloved's only sibling. She stared the whole time at some spot just above my head, creating the illusion of connection. Being near Corey felt like standing in the wings of an X-rated circus act — which no doubt heightened my brother's affections for her. She was a living collector's piece: rock memorabilia in the making.

Matthew and Corey cuddled up on a loveseat and fidgeted as we talked, chain wallets and boot buckles rattling. Clad from head to night sitcoms. He locked himself in the bathroom, letting me in only after I promised not to tell anyone he'd been hurt. The heel of his black Converse high-top was severed, the bloody stump of flesh shining through. I called a family friend who was a nurse for help, defying my brother for one of the few times I can recall. I remember our nurse friend filling the tub with warm water, and how Matthew screamed when she immersed his foot, and how, though he went to the ER, we never spoke of it and I never saw his heel again, though after that he must have been a permanent kind of off-balance.

I told him the story as I remembered it, to see if it was real.

"Yeah," he said. "Hurt like hell, but it happened." His smile captured what I can only describe as old joy. "It all happened."

Then he got real quiet in that way he did when he had something to say. "Did you hear about the letter Aunt Lisa sent me?"

I could tell this was a test to see if the letter was common knowledge in the family. It was not.

"A letter about what?" The only mail I ever received from her arrived on my birthday — a Hallmark card and a twenty, on time, every year.

"It was a big ole handwritten letter about how she knows I'm on drugs and she's scared I'm going to die." His chin crimped up in shame for a moment. He stared at his hands to steady himself.

"Who's saying that stuff, Missy? Is that what Mom's telling everyone? That I'm just some fucked-up junkie?"

He looked right at me, and I looked right at the floor.

That's exactly what Mom had said. To her sisters on the phone, to me, to our father. Our mother had raised us to understand it was impolite to say what you really think to someone's face. Like all of us, she was scared and dealing with a situation she had no idea how to fix. Matthew stayed away from us for lengthening stretches, and came back changed. We could all tell drugs were part of that equation, but I couldn't stand to injure him by owning it.

toe in black leather and denim, they looked misplaced in the burgundy and beige hotel room.

Uninterested in our mother's agenda of ironing out details for
tomorrow's ceremony, Matthew pulled a list of baby names from
his wallet—which scared even Mom, who wanted to be a grandmother more than she ever wanted to be a mother. *Cisco* topped
the name list. *Little Cisco,* they said, as if she or he were a real child
who existed in some rose-tinted future.

"But you guys aren't actually pregnant, right?" Mom said.

"No. Just collecting names. For when." Then they tongue-kissed
in front of us.

Since the summer of '86 when Matthew lost his virginity at age
fourteen with our childhood friend Erron Star, I'd not known him
to be without a girlfriend. Women were some kind of sweet spot
where he felt most like himself. What cars were to me, perhaps.

That was the summer my father paid two vagrant men a small
sum to reroof our house. Rog and Dewey came to work late each
day and labored through the heat in highwater plaid pants and
button-down shirts from the Salvation Army. I'd sit on the lawn or
float in the pool, keeping a wide berth around the house because
of the asphalt shingles they tossed to the ground without warning. Though Rog and Dewey took smoke breaks every hour or so,
making small talk with me, it was Matthew they most enjoyed. He
enjoyed them right back, adopting their curse words and dialect—
the accent a hybrid of tooth loss, rural roots, and hard living.

One day, Matthew called up to the roof, "Guys. I got a dead pos-
sum."

Their heads appeared over the soffit, all sweat and sunburn.

"Whatcha gonna do with it?"

"I don't know. I'm busy, and it's hot out."

"We'll take it." Rog and Dewey climbed down the ladder and claimed the carcass.

Matthew and Dad deliberated over dinner about whether the men wanted the meat, the skin, or both. Matthew intended to give it to them all along, but offering directly would have been an insult.

Between Erron and Rog and Dewey, Matthew made some big decisions about what it meant to be a man that summer. Years later, Erron confessed he was the love of her life, a sentiment I heard about my brother from more women than I can count on both hands, though I remember them all. I studied them, trying to nail down what they had that I didn't — the things that made them special. There was Jennifer Jones, who shared her name with a movie star. And Natalie the quiet punk rocker, who had spent most of her life in Germany before her father took a position at the nearby military base, Camp Atterbury. Then Justine, the red-head with the ferret who somehow talked Matthew into going to prom. Next, Kim — the girl I'd driven to the jail the summer of the Turd. And Jenny Irene, the one who'd lost her front teeth defending Matthew during the Vincennes Incident. The one who claimed he cooked her shrimp bisque using a Dutch oven on the roof of his boarding house during the dog days of summer. The only girl I know of that he impregnated — he became engaged to her, then moved all the way to Athens when she miscarried. In Georgia he met Krista, the sweet southern girl with pigtails and penciled-on eyebrows. And finally Corey. There were others in between, over-laps but never gaps.

Jenny Irene once told me, "Last time I saw Matt, I was pregnant with my second and holding a toddler on my lap. He was back vis-iting Columbus, maybe the Christmas before he died. He smiled at me and said I was the hottest-looking pregnant woman he'd ever seen. Then he leaned in and whispered, *You're still in love with me, aren't you?* I didn't say anything. I was married, you know. He leaned in again and said, *Me too.* And that's it. That's the last time I saw him."

I couldn't help but envy Jenny. After all, she'd lost her front grill trying to save my brother, and all I had to show for myself was a handful of never-read poems, built on a shaky foundation of angst and worry.

> *Consider this: Dad's seed never found Mom's egg because when his ex-girlfriend painted a sunset on his trunk they reunited. Mom became a model, Dad motorcycled across the country with the Other Girl's arms around his waist, and Matthew stepped to the rear of the life line, took a new number, and felt nothing at all.*

In the summer of '96 I flew to Indiana to visit our folks for a week then borrowed the Honda to drive down to Athens and see Matthew. He'd taken a job as a garbage man and couldn't get time off to come to Indiana, so I came to him.

Around dusk, I pulled up to the house he shared with roommates. Matthew sat on the front porch steps, beer in hand, waiting for me. We rarely spent time just the two of us. I was tickled to see him but felt awkward when I noticed the new tattoo at the base of his neck, just above his shirt collar. It was a banner with an almost-finished name — exactly one space, followed by the letters *E-L-I-S-S-A.*

He saw me see the tattoo. We blushed the same blush and averted our eyes — a learned response to intimacy or conflict that runs in our family. I mentioned the humidity. He handed me a beer, which I sipped to busy myself. He took a deep breath, looked down at a greening band on his left ring finger and spun it around.

"Don't tell Mom," he said, "but I got married." He grinned at me like this was the start of a far richer story.

"You did?"

He pulled an envelope out of his back pocket and showed me the name on the return address, written in bubbly, middle-schooler lettering: *Elissa Stephenson*. My name minus a single letter.

"Met her last month. She's a stripper. From Kentucky. Has a kid, she says. We got married and she's trying to work things out with the kid's dad so she can move down here."

Questions flooded my brain and stalled it out.

"I got her name tattooed right here." He ran his fingers over the banner.

"Where did you get married?"

"We walked over to the courthouse one night."

I guessed then what I would find out four years later, at the courthouse in Athens, the day we collected his personal belongings from the police: There was no marriage certificate.

"You got rings?"

"Yeah. From a candy machine. We'll get real ones soon."

I still had no idea what to say. "I mean, wow. Congratulations?"

He cracked another beer, and tapped the tattoo as he spoke. "I left a space in front of her name so I can change it to my sister's name, you know, in case things don't work out."

That's what he'd been waiting for — the punch line. We laughed. When I saw him next, that banner held my name, and we never mentioned Elissa again.

The first time I heard about Corey, Matthew was shit-talking her. It was the start of 1998, and he called to tell me his friends' band had a tour stop in Missoula, and Josh and I should go see the show. "Tell Ruyter and Blaine you know me, and they'll buy you a drink," he said.

I knew this routine. As soon as I announced myself as Matthew Stephenson's little sister, people looked on me with equal parts admiration and confusion. Exactly how was this pint-size wallflower genetically linked to a guy who lit up a room like a Christmas tree? Regardless, Matthew's friends always told me two things: how highly he spoke of me, and how much they loved him.

Matthew had one more thing to say about the situation. "Stay away from the fire-breathing Amazon Corey Parks," he said. "She's a no-talent whore. A real fucking cunt. But everyone else is great."

It was rare for my brother to speak so harshly of someone unless they'd wronged him. In his youth he kept the Bulldozer List. When someone committed an unforgivable offense, their name went on the list. Though I'm certain I once occupied the top ten slots for various offenses ("borrowing" his ACDC cassette, touching his Animal Muppet, attempting to make eye contact), I might be the only offender Matthew ever granted pardon. My brother loved hard, but he held a grudge like a dog guards a bone. So it came as no real surprise when his ex-girlfriend Krista later told me Matthew had crashed and burned their relationship by sleeping with Corey right after proposing to Krista. Then Corey had turned around and slept with someone else. Though my brother could dish out infidelity, the same treatment came as a shock to him.

I had to work during Nashville Pussy's first Missoula show, but Josh went. Word on the street was Corey had slept with one of our local musician friends. When his oral sex performance was not to her liking, she said, *Lick it, man, don't bite it,* and threatened to punch him in the face. Three months later, my brother and Corey Parks were engaged, traveling the world on Nashville Pussy's tour.

While we all sensed Corey was deadly as a midnight tornado in a trailer park, we also knew why he wanted her. Our home state provided us few role models for success and fame. We used stories to forge nearness to our handful of notable Hoosiers. David Letterman had picked up a family friend who was hitchhiking. John Cougar Mellencamp's mother had kissed me on the head when I was a baby. Matthew went to high school with Nascar star Tony Stewart, who he said was a real nice guy. Axl Rose and his bandmate Izzy Stradlin hailed from Lafayette, a detail that did not escape us when *Appetite for Destruction* dominated the airwaves. The Jacksons gave us our unofficial state anthem, "Goin' Back to Indiana," which was far better than our official anthem, "On the Banks of the Wabash." Florence Henderson from *The Brady Bunch* was a Hoosier, Shelley Long from *Cheers,* and Steve McQueen, even, who could rock a shawl-collar cardigan and smoke a cigarette while driving a Mustang Fastback (a stick shift at that) through the hilly streets of San Francisco. Billboards along the highway memorialized the birthplace of James Dean. We suffered through Dan Quayle while celebrating Larry Bird back in the days when no one knew a lick about Mike Pence. We had Jim Davis, the creator of Garfield, and Kurt Vonnegut (my father's favorite famous Hoosier). It never surprised me that Amelia Earhart, Wilbur Wright, and Gus Grissom (the second man to fly in space) all sprang from my home state. Indiana instilled in me such a deep need for flight that their stories offered comfort.

By the time Matthew met Corey, it was clear no branch of our family tree would graze fame and fortune. My brother and I were wanderers, too busy pioneering life beyond state lines to get ahead. Matthew must have seen in Corey the culmination of his greatest loves: rock 'n' roll, questionable behavior, and powerful women.

Dad once traveled to Chicago to watch a Nashville Pussy show with Matthew, who worked as an undercover security guard of sorts. Dad hung in the audience with Matthew until he spotted some dude trying to climb on stage to get to Corey. Matthew handed Dad his beer, said, "Be right back," then crowd-surfed to the stage, held the man by his shirt collar while punching him, then returned to Dad's side, his knuckles bloody as he reclaimed his beer.

With the band, Matthew saw Europe, visited most of the States, and even attended the Grammys. In a phone call after his one and only red carpet experience, he told me two things: *Those famous people are real tiny. Like, Madonna is small as you, Missy.* And, my favorite detail, *I even saw Lucinda Williams. She was the most beautiful woman there.* I took this as acknowledgment that Corey was image over substance, a caricature of a human that could have sprung entirely from the depths of my brother's preteen dreams — no more, no less.

When we read in *Spin* magazine Corey's quote, "My husband got my name tattooed on his penis. Now that's love . . ." we knew he'd finally reached the ranks of infamy he'd always wanted. Though I never witnessed it, her name, it turned out, *was* etched on the top of his member, flanked by a lightning bolt on each side. Before he died he told us he covered up Corey's name by tattooing the word *hard* above his patch, leaving *core* on his shaft, and turning the *y* into the top of Jesus's head. The mouth went around his urethra so (he chuckled as he said it) *Each time I piss it looks like Jesus is puking up beer.*

Two days before the wedding we stopped by Matthew and Corey's house to see a table Aunt Beth had given them. A beautiful early-sixties Chevy truck sat in the drive — my brother's, I remembered, navy with cream-colored streaks on each side. I could tell by the collection of dead leaves on the hood and the lack of tracks in the mud that it hadn't been driven since they left on tour. On a previous trip to Athens he'd driven me around town in it, searching out a place to cash his paycheck. A natural-born libertarian, he avoided bank accounts and resented paying taxes.

Corey's car sat next to the Chevy. She'd bought a late-model Jetta, forest green, nicer than any car Matthew or I had ever owned.

Inside their house, the first thing I noticed were the seven-foot ceilings — short enough that Corey had to duck under doorways. We gathered around the giant table from Pier 1 Imports that looked awkwardly upscale in a room full of scavenged furniture.

Matthew picked up the Ball jar centerpiece and held it to the light. Inside, a black spider with a leg span broad as a half-dollar hung from a corner of web she'd spun.

"I didn't know she was going to have babies when I caught her." Matthew flicked the glass to spark some action. Little black specks scattered around the mother. A piece of paper towel lined the top of the jar, letting in air. A red violin marked the mother's back.

"I gave her rocks and a twig, crickets to eat, then she laid eggs. Now there's all these babies and shit." He set the jar down, and I ran my finger along the edge of the table, as thick and heavy as a chopping block.

"Aunt Beth says it seats eight." He sounded suspicious of the table, as I was the spiders.

"Nice," I said.

"Yep."

"I don't cook," Corey said. "But we eat a whole lot of fried chicken." She squeezed between us to regard the table, her rib cage level with my shoulders. "Fuckin' sweet, though, huh?"

My brother and I nodded. Her own album cover hung on the wall nearby, showing her and the other female band member with men's heads between their legs. *Let Them Eat Pussy,* it said. Our mother seemed not to notice.

I kept looking at the table, thinking how when you get married people give you things, how I worked two jobs and had a college degree and a dog and a boyfriend and owned nothing as nice as this table with a black widow centerpiece.

"How was the drive down?" Matthew asked, meaning the stretch we'd driven in Mom's Honda, from Columbus to Georgia.

"Fine," I said, choosing not to mention how I blew by a cop going ninety, slammed on the brakes, and almost got us rear-ended.

It still bothered me a day later, the thought of our near miss, for the same reason I could never have slept in their house, with that spider spinning her web all night long, only a thin skin of paper between us.

Consider this: Your brother didn't die because Jenny Irene never miscarried. They married in the spring of 1993 and, together, raised Cannon and Harley in Brown County — a half-dozen miles from Betty and Don's.

The wedding took place at the infamous 40 Watt Club in Athens. Called "the 40" by locals, this music venue (owned by a member of R.E.M.) hosted some of the best local and national music. Matthew attended it the way most southerners attended church. He worked the desk at the tattoo parlor next door, owned by his Indiana friends — a pair of identical twins.

Corey's mother brought her sewing machine on the plane all the way from California to fashion her daughter a white version of a Morticia Addams dress right there in the hotel, the midriff cinched together with a white corset, topped off with a crown of calla lilies for her hair.

That night before the wedding, I visited Watson, one of the "Twins of Pain" at the tattoo parlor. He inscribed a black tribal banner beneath my collarbones, my own design. I hadn't told Matthew. I wanted it to be a surprise. It went beautifully with the black off-the-shoulder cocktail dress Corey had chosen for her bridesmaids.

I stood through the ceremony the next day, my new tattoo shiny under a layer of antibiotic ointment, trying not to smear the eye makeup I never wore in real life. Matthew sported a vintage tuxedo with a Volaré-blue ruffled shirt — a sophisticated version of his childhood dress-up shenanigans. He'd loved to visit the local Salvation Army with his friends and create ensembles of old-man loafers and too-small polyester pants (inspired by Rog and Dewey), or perhaps coveralls (the uniform of our step-grandpa Don Chaney). Then he and his friends would skateboard through the neighborhood in what Matthew called their "Gorman outfits." He lived like life was a performance of sorts, and his wedding was no exception.

After the vows, the party ensued.

We held on to tradition as best we could, all of us standing in a circle, watching the newlyweds sway in time. Matthew danced with Mom next, and our father with Corey. Finally Uncle Mark pushed me toward the center of the circle. I stumbled on my two-inch heels. Matthew and I faced each other. Neither of us knew what to do other than rock back and forth while standing as far from each other as possible, faces averted.

"This is the only slow dance I know," he said. "I call it the Prom. Justine showed me how in twelfth grade."

I laughed. "I got a new tattoo," I said.

"Yep." He donned a tense smile.

His response rattled me. I didn't yet understand that tattoos weren't something he wanted for me, that he never intended to be my role model. Matthew cut the tension the best way he knew how: with a fart joke or two.

Once the dances ended, he and Corey disappeared for a couple hours, getting high, we all guessed, in the green room, to celebrate their good fortune.

Uncle Mark, by then pleasantly drunk on Irish whiskey, put one hand on my shoulder and his other on Josh's, and asked when we planned on taking the leap. Josh looked sweet and dapper in a fedora and vintage gray sport coat. I loved him, and the idea that we, too, could play house blossomed in my head like a volunteer flower. Josh dodged the question by going for another round.

Near the end of the night my voice grew louder under the influence of too much champagne. Drunk, I searched for Corey, planning to call her *sister* and give her a hug. Aunt Beth told me Corey had gone off, god knows where. She looked toward the center of the dance floor where, hours earlier, my brother had wed.

"She's not going to leave him standing," Beth said, shaking her head back and forth.

I stared back at her, wondering how she could say that. How she could pretend to know such a thing.

The next day, we said goodbye to Matthew and Corey in front of our hotel. They waved as they climbed into Corey's Jetta with the tinted windows, and I realized I'd forgotten to ask Matthew what was up with the Chevy. It was the same kind of vehicle our own parents had driven when they'd gotten hitched way back in '71, after a wedding where people cried the wrong kind of tears. No one believed in them, their future, or the idea of Matthew and me. We didn't want to repeat the same mistake by not believing in Matthew and the life he chose. The least we could do was offer up our good faith, to remain loving and open-minded.

One drive and two flights later, Josh and I landed back in Montana, leaving Matthew to pass his nights under a too-low roof with Corey, the Chevy, and those lethal creatures in a Ball jar on the dining table.

THIRTEEN

The Majesty of the Seas

Miami: October 1999

*I*N *SPRING OF 1999,* just months after Matthew's wedding, I convinced Josh to marry me while sharing a post-work six-pack and watching an *I Love Lucy* marathon. We had just finished a three-day run of twelve-hour shifts at the group homes. He worked the boys' house, and I worked the girls'. We were paid to modify the behavior of children who'd endured unthinkable abuses. That day a rotund ten-year-old had tried to stab me with a piece of jagged glass — a weapon she'd fashioned by shattering a frame that held a picture of one of her many foster mothers. Angel — the child — suffered the only injury: a cut hand.

I cried and laughed while we watched *Lucy,* advancing my argument for marriage during commercial breaks in ways I didn't yet see as manipulative.

"We want to be together forever, right?"

Josh regarded my question as if it were rhetorical.

"And, like you said, it's just a piece of paper. So why not? If it hardly matters anyway. If you love me like that already."

When Josh saw I'd dug my heels in, he put an arm around me and said, "Okay then."

By the time we went to bed, I'd agreed to take his last name, and he was chuckling over the idea of us "getting hitched."

Vegas was our Plan A. Two years earlier, we'd driven down for my cousin Chad's wedding. Before the Athens ceremony, Matthew and Corey had eloped in Vegas while wearing giant sombreros. If we wed there as well, we'd help set a new family tradition. We pooled all of our cash. I smoothed, stacked, and counted bills, made piles of change, but no matter how many times I tallied, the total came out the same: four hundred and forty dollars. Enough for Vegas only if we slept in the van.

Later that same week, I received my favorite kind of letter in the mail, the kind the twelve-year-old inside me still covets above all else: an acceptance. I'd been granted a two-month residency at Vermont Studio Center, a place writers and visual artists go to have time and space to hone their craft. The residency made no practical sense. I'd have to quit my jobs and raise three thousand dollars for my portion of the fees to spend two cold, dark months in the Northeast. I also knew it would take grave injury to keep me from it.

The next day, my mother called.

"I just booked us on a cruise leaving in October, on your birthday — the seventeenth," she said. "Can you believe that?"

"Gross." I'd been giving her shit about her cruising habit for years. "Have fun dumping your trash in the ocean."

"You're going, too. Our gift. I put down a deposit on two rooms. One for us, and one for you and Josh. The deposit is non-refundable." The lilt fell sharply from her voice as she repeated, "Non-re-fundable."

Okay then.

Plan B was born. I called up the cruise line and booked our onboard nuptials. We would marry in U.S. waters on the morning of departure, the morning of my twenty-fifth birthday, on a cruise boat called the *Majesty of the Seas*. The dates aligned flawlessly: departing on my birthday and arriving stateside the day I was due in Vermont. In the meantime, I saved every spare dollar to pay for my writing residency. Either it was all meant to be, or it was a perfect storm. (To this day, I believe it was both.)

In a local vintage shop I found the only wedding dress that interested me: a 1960s ankle-length brocade sheath with a ballet neckline and three-quarter sleeves, to cover my tattoos. Two-dozen fabric-covered buttons lined the spine. A detachable train hung from the shoulders like an Audrey Hepburn superhero cape. I tried it on and opened the dressing room curtain so the store owner could zip me in.

"Look at that." She crossed her arms and nodded. "I never thought this dress would find a bride tiny enough."

The sleeves were sewn so snugly in their sockets that I could only make arm motions from the elbows down. Still, I had never felt so lovely.

The week I found the dress, Matthew and Corey blew through town on a tour stop with Nashville Pussy. They looked like feral castaways rescued from an island decades after shipwreck. It was Matthew's first visit to Missoula. He admired my dogs while Corey stared at the floor, rubbing her hands over her face again and again, one knee bopping up and down as if keeping time to a death metal soundtrack. She paused only to shake her head like a horse twitching off flies.

I thought we'd have a day together. I'd prepared a list of things to do: lunch, a scenic drive and a hike, then happy hour at a hole-in-the-wall bar with cheap drinks and a pool table. I'd hoped to fit in a trip to the vintage shop to show my new sister-in-law the dress, but the two of them fell asleep in the back room, waking only hours before showtime.

I took them to dinner at Charlie B's (the bar where I had met Josh and learned to drink), then off to the show. I stood near the back of the crowd, my brother on one side and my soon-to-be husband on the other, watching Corey breathe fire and make out with the other gal in the band, both of them stripped down to bras.

As I watched, I thought about what Corey was and what I was not, some insight trying to hatch in my brain about the line between positive and negative attention, power and exploitation, human and object. But the sound waves from the giant amps dissembled all thought. Corey lit up the stage, so filled with energy that she seemed capable of levitation. One of my group home coworkers — a graduate student who met the world with a chronic frown — threw her own bra on stage.

At home after bar time, Matthew fed my blue heeler champagne from a plastic cup. We watched her chase the tennis ball, talking about how wonderful Dad could be if he'd just break his work addiction and regulate his diabetes. We talked about Mom. She had graduated to a stage of drinking where my father would put her to bed by nine if she didn't excuse herself, and it was not uncommon to find her walking barefoot over the shards of a wineglass she'd just broken, unaware she'd cut herself, her foot trailing blood across beige tile.

"She's drinking herself to death," Matthew said. "It's happening right now."

We traded stories about events I wasn't sure were real anymore — dead pets, the color of the shag carpeting in the first house we ever lived in, Matthew coming home one night when I was twelve and our parents out to dinner, his right heel cut clean off. He'd run from a party the cops raided, jumping out a window onto a stack of storm windows buried under fall leaves below. He'd limped through the back door with a sock tied around his right foot while I sat in front of the TV with the JCPenney catalogue and my Saturday-

"No one's saying you're a fucked-up addict," I told him, hiding behind semantics. Instead, they said *in trouble,* or *into drugs.* "They just see you guys living this crazy life and you don't come home much and everyone gets worried, is all."

"Aunt Lisa said she loves me even though I'm a drug addict." He shook his head back and forth in disbelief.

Aunt Lisa had been like a second mother to us. She didn't have her own child until I was five, so she and our Uncle Tom would take us overnight, buy us toys and clothes, let us eat too much candy and watch all the TV. In the morning, Lisa cooked us scrambled eggs in bacon grease. Tom would come home from the night shift in his police uniform and the two of them would sing to each other their favorite song, "You've Lost That Lovin' Feeling." For Aunt Lisa to think Matthew an addict must have leveled one of the oldest, most primitive parts of his heart.

Though he shared with me his anger and hurt, he didn't deny using. Unlike me, he couldn't bring himself to lie. I didn't then think of my whitewashed words as deceit. I simply couldn't imagine telling a truth that would hurt the feelings of someone I loved — Matthew above all.

Consider this: The Mustang blew a tire on the road to Arizona. Your folks rolled six times and never came home. You were never born and Matthew was orphaned, raised by Aunt Lisa in the county your parents escaped.

In the morning, we waited on the front porch for the tour bus to pick them up. They were off to another gig in another town.

"I'm gonna try and make your wedding, Missy. I am." We shared one of those wide-armed hugs where you kind of pat each other on the back without touching bodies.

Corey snuggled up to him and spoke in a baby voice that turned my stomach. "But we'll be on tour, love. I can't tour without my road manager." Then she looked at me. "What a bummer, honey."

Matthew smiled nervously, and I knew then he wouldn't make it.

I held out a box of the granola cereal the pair of them lived off — a thing I'd bought for them to enjoy during his visit, thinking there would be more time. "You should take this."

"Shit, Missy. Thanks."

I never went back to see the Audrey dress. I choose instead to have something made from a plain-Jane pattern bought at the local fabric store. My wedding would be such a negligible happening that I couldn't even find someone to go dress shopping with me. It felt like a nonevent already. A story of my own invention. Though the dress had fit perfectly, I felt suddenly and entirely too small for it.

A hurricane ravaged Miami in the two days leading up to the ceremony. After a long and chaotic boat-boarding process during which we weren't sure we'd set sail, an attendant ushered me, solo, to our room.

"You'd better hurry," she said. "The wedding is in fifteen minutes." She made a clicking sound with her tongue and shut the door behind her.

I took a moment to undo my modest expectations of our accommodations. What the cruise line called a cabin looked more like a large closet, with a bed and a bathroom so tiny that you could sit on the toilet and brush your teeth over the sink while washing your feet in the shower. Summoning my best eye-of-the-storm calm, I managed to strip, shower, shave, and dry my hair in less than ten minutes.

Mom and the wedding officiant arrived, cramming themselves

into the room. I stood in my undergarments — arms held out cru-
cifixion-style — as they dressed me.

The officiant had a British accent, spectacles, knee-high hose,
and black orthopedic shoes. As she read our vows aloud, I regret-
ted including Nietzsche's ideas about the Eternal Return — that
our lives recur in their exact specificity for all of time. In a universe that revolves around the Eternal Return, we were getting
married and had been getting married and would always be mar-
rying, over and over, like a movie playing on repeat. Though we'd
lifted the quotes in our vows from *The Unbearable Lightness of Being* — a novel I'd previously considered romantic — the words felt
more heavy than eloquent, each sentence an anchor instead of a
buoy.

The cruise brochure I'd studied for the past few months pic-
tured a bride descending the three-story spiral staircase at the
center of the boat to meet her groom. When my father fetched me
from the elevator, he led us past this staircase and stopped near a
pair of red doors in a low-ceilinged hallway.

"It's the cigar lounge," Dad said. He shrugged his shoulders the
way he might over a hotel room with mildew on the ceiling and
curly hairs in the tub. "I guess the wedding's in there."

The room was red as the inside of a uterus. Red carpet covered the floors, and a fleet of red leather sofas faced the back of the
room, where Josh and the wedding party stood, waiting for me.
Pachelbel's *Canon in D* played at speaker-crackling volume on a
portable CD player in the corner.

*If every second of our lives recurs an infinite number of times, we
are nailed to eternity as Jesus Christ was nailed to the cross.*

I wanted to back slowly out of that womb-room, but then I saw
Josh, my best friend, his expression a perfect mix of wonder, humor, and love. An expression that made me feel loved and visible.

My bargain-basement dreams for an under-the-radar wedding had become a cautionary tale. The only way through was forward. Because everyone knows how the wedding story ends: with *I dos* and cheers and an open bar.

In the world of eternal return the weight of unbearable responsibility lies heavy on every move we make . . .

The boat photographer's shutter clicked over and over like a lone paparazzi. I couldn't even look at the half-dozen relatives who'd made it on board (some had not), or the few bridesmaids or groomsmen who cast their best fake smiles my way.

If eternal return is the heaviest of burdens, then our lives can stand out against it in all their splendid lightness.

I'd nearly forgotten the date: October 17. My birthday. I tried not to think about the hurricane as some kind of omen, about how Matthew would have rendered this scene comedy instead of tragedy.

Josh and I locked eyes and held hands — the two of us sporting bad haircuts and reasonable doubt. The vows, I hoped, would turn our love into something more solid, something we could lean on.

Okay then.

I married him anyway.

Shortly after the ceremony, the ship set sail and the drinking commenced. I downed a bottle of champagne, mustered in an orange life jacket and my wedding dress, and cried about the hurricane, a wrinkled dress, my absent brother, and my bright future as a wife. We changed for dinner, drank more, and passed out face-down in our miniature bedroom before ten. When Josh got up the next morning, I noticed a brown smear on his side of the bed. He saw it as well and checked his boxers in horror, fearing some drunken accident involving his own feces. Then I spotted the Andes Candy wrapper stuck to the sheets. *Thank god.* Our wedding had been an unalterable fiasco, but at least no one had shat the bed.

I soon realized another grave error in my do-it-yourself wedding planning: We would spend the duration of our honeymoon with twenty of our closest family members on a boat the size of a modest shopping mall. During that week, I ran on a treadmill that faced giant windows at the back of the boat — the water rolling away from me and I ran toward it, an experience so disorienting I suffered seasickness for the rest of the trip. Dad shamed Mom for her drinking after she danced to the Y.M.C.A. song at dinner. She walked around for two days afterward with a wineglass in hand, sipping alone and talking to no one. All the while the cruise band scored our family drama by playing on repeat the only song they seemed to know: "Who Let the Dogs Out." *Woof. Woof. Woof woof.*

Food poisoning set in the day we disembarked. Some of my family members who had eaten on the islands became so ill they couldn't stand. The airline attendants upgraded my mother to first class on her flight back to Indiana, clearing an entire row for her in fear of contagion. I disembarked without injury, grateful to be back in the states and bound for Vermont. I waved goodbye to everyone, Josh included, and headed off for my two-month residency. It was the perfect antidote to the weight of matrimony, the proximity of family, and the song lyrics I'd later come to learn were code for "Who let the ugly bitches into the club?"

On my birthday, during the wedding reception and after her first bottle of wine, my mother told me that Matthew had called days earlier and asked to attend the ceremony. His plan was to fly down, board the boat for the wedding, and disembark before we set sail. (I'd cleared this plan with the cruise line months ago.) It would have worked. When he called Mom at the eleventh hour to accept her offer of a plane ticket, she refused.

"I told him it was too late," she said on the deck of that boat, as the sun set over the Atlantic. "I told him too bad. It's time for some tough love."

There are some things in life you know are mistakes when you're doing them. Perhaps our mother knew this about her tough love the way I knew this about my marriage. My pride had tricked me into making the worst kind of decision. It wasn't that I didn't love Josh. (I did, as much as I knew how to love anyone.) But I had no business getting hitched. I needed to stretch and expand, find the edges of myself and cross every state line. I needed open road, not a traditional life. I needed to listen to my own voice instead of surrounding myself with others who shouted their needs loudly, without hesitation.

Matthew needed medical care, not a random set of boundaries Mom dredged up from a long-ago episode of *The Phil Donahue Show*. He needed support, diagnoses, intervention.

Instead he got cut out of my wedding, left to drift in his own dark waters.

Consider this: Your parents said yes to rehab and your brother lived five more years, mostly sober, until one Tuesday in February when he drank all the Night Train and swallowed all the pills and left you his dog, his truck, and his three-year-old daughter, Lucinda.

FOURTEEN

Porsche 944

Vermont and Indiana: 1999

*F*ALL IN VERMONT CAME as welcome antidote to our Caribbean nuptials. The leaves lit the sky with fiery colors the week I arrived. Soon, I woke to stark branches silhouetted against white. Perhaps because I was born in October, because I am part old lady, because I adore bitter beer and fine yarn, I feel most at home in the fall. Everything dies, disintegrates, lets go. The trick is to lean into this ending, meet it with awe instead of fear, to accept that the cold and isolation of deep snow and small spaces waits around the bend. It's a time of year when each day becomes more valuable, darkening too quickly into the next.

The artists' retreat I'd flown to in Vermont was structured to keep daily life simple and minimize distractions. We had no Internet, though such a thing played a nominal role in my life in the fall of '99. I'd only had an email address for a couple of years, and cell phones were new gadgets for the business class. We had solitude and books and time to make art or, in my case, time to churn out half-baked short stories for my graduate school applications.

Vermont Studio Center — or VSC, as locals called it — was located in the town of Johnson. I had no car there, so I took up running again as a way to explore the terrain. I ran through the few blocks of businesses the locals called "town," through the leaves and soon the snow, up the hill to the university, and down through the graveyard. As the solstice neared, I had to finish running by four-thirty or I'd find myself in the dark. I stopped at a graveyard at dusk one day to look at the headstones, and I noticed the word "relict" on the grave of a woman dated around the turn of the century. Instead of *dead,* she was *relict* — defunct, irrelevant, useless. I had felt relict my whole life, somehow, like a bird perched on a branch outside a stranger's window, looking in.

I walked over to the main building and up the stairs once every few days to call Josh or check in with my folks. Often I had to wait in line for the single phone all the artists shared, which sat in a room the size of a closet (or a cruise boat cabin). You could close the door for privacy and gaze out the window at the river rushing below. It's possible I called home primarily for the view. I rarely had much to say. Nothing happened. I was silent and sometimes surly — bad phone company, like back in the days of Interlochen.

During one call I learned that a friend had found Matthew passed out on the floor with a loaded shotgun pressed into his neck and a syringe in his arm. Apparently when things went south with Corey, he'd returned to Athens to dissemble their shared rental house with the low, low ceilings. I can only imagine his shame and frustration after overdosing just enough to stop him from pulling the trigger.

Our mother was irate, mistaking Matthew's despair for a personal attack.

"What is he trying to pull?" she said.

The trigger, I thought, though I let the question remain rhetorical.

Matthew went to the hospital and even asked to go to rehab, something my folks would have to pay for out-of-pocket. Asking for help does not come naturally to any branch of our family tree. Pride held Matthew in such a tight grasp that if you wanted him to take something, even something he desperately needed, you'd have to insist three times over, avoid eye contact, assure him it was no skin off your back, then leave the item and walk away. Maybe it would vanish. Maybe it wouldn't. Asking my parents to float the bill for rehab, I imagine, cut to bone.

What I remember most about that call is the cadence of my father's speech. He spoke slowly, like a man sensing a storm that's not yet hatched.

"When I talked to him, you know what he said? I told him to get a place, get a car, get a job, quit the junk, and get some rest. He said, 'It's like I have two broken legs and you keep asking me to walk.'"

Our conversation ended in silence, punctuated by my father's irregular breathing as he tried to bring himself back from tears.

We cried. We feared. We reasoned and worried. But no one paid for rehab.

Matthew stayed in the hospital long enough to detox. We heard that Corey flew in from L.A. shortly after the incident. In a harbinger of things to come, she checked them both in to a hotel in Atlanta for two weeks, then left him for good. He did what he could in her absence: joined AA, got the job at the landfill, moved into the trailer, found a new girl, and bought the Ford.

I have two broken legs and you keep asking me to walk.

I did the only thing I knew how to do: I built a poem around those words in the days that followed, as if margins and line breaks could give such a dangerous sentiment boundaries and edges; a beginning and a middle without end.

Consider this: Your brother didn't die in Georgia but joined the circus as an illustrated man, incinerated in his sleep after smoking in bed one crisp, clear night in Nebraska.

I have no memory of Matthew's last Christmas. I left Vermont on December 22, 1999, and flew back to Montana to spend the holiday with Josh. We fell into our normal rhythm, relieved to have our wedding fiasco and two-month separation behind us. When left to our own devices, we rarely had problems. We liked being together — eating, drinking, sleeping, not sleeping. That Christmas felt like our real honeymoon — a private holiday in the town we loved. We'd duck into a bar for hazelnut liquor, kick the snow off our boots, then walk down to the Wilma for a movie, or go see a band play at Jay's Upstairs, a dodgy second-floor venue where the floor bowed under the weight of the crowd.

Before New Year's, I flew solo to my folks' place while Josh hung back for work. If he were free, we would have driven the van together and brought the dogs.

I walked down the stairs with bags in hand to find Matthew anchoring the couch to the basement floor. "Hey," I said.

He took a minute to focus. It was the first time I'd seen him since he'd visited Missoula with the band the summer before.

"Oh. Hey. Missy." No trace of a smile. He looked tapped, drained, lucky to be alive.

"Here for a visit?" I asked.

"I got a ride up to take Dad's car." He looked at me finally. "He's giving me the Porsche."

The Porsche was opposite the sort of ride either of us would want. I'm sure Matthew felt about the car the way I felt about Mom's Honda. Would he even fit in such a low rider? I couldn't think of a thing to say.

On the drive home from the airport, Dad had mentioned only that Matthew *seemed to be having a hard time.* Mom complained that he wouldn't talk to her. I got the feeling that everyone knew the true reason for his visit except me. The Porsche and what else? I never thought to ask directly.

Like an animal conserving resources, Matthew barely moved. He sat on the sofa, leaning forward, elbows on knees, hands clasped, eyes set vacantly on the Stainmaster carpet. He wore his usual uniform: Levi's, steel-toe work boots, quilted flannel, concert T-shirt, and a black baseball hat (bill forward) concealing unwashed hair. Something about him flickered — a flame inside a jar.

I knew we had to help him, but I didn't know how. We'd almost lost him to that shotgun and syringe incident in November (an event no one mentioned). I couldn't leave him alone, which is what he seemed to want. But approaching him while he was in this much pain felt like dragging back a dog that's gone off to die. I did all I could think to do — a simple yet incredibly difficult action: I sat next to him, on that dingy white sectional we'd spent our younger years ruining, shaped vaguely like a fingernail moon. And I kept sitting, terrified he'd ask me to leave. He didn't.

We sat there sober for three days straight with a fully stocked bar at our backs. Sometimes one of us would turn on the television for white noise. Sometimes I changed the channel. Sometimes he lowered his face to his hands for a half-hour or longer then lifted it again to the carpet.

I forgot to think about me, about my own life. I was on the verge of change again — a newlywed filling envelopes with graduate school applications ready to be mailed off to far parts of the country. I was ready to move, ready to write, and I hoped my husband was ready too. All my goals and dreams and plans evaporated as I sat with Matthew, humbled by my inability to help him.

Mom checked on us regularly, unnerved by our strange and silent vigil. The longer we sat, the more agitated she appeared.

Recent Christmases had already become emotional minefields in that house. Mom clearly suffered from obsession. She joked often that she was a compulsive house cleaner. While it's true that her carpets often wore out from excessive vacuuming, and it's also true that she got tendinitis from said vacuuming, her behaviors reeked of anxiety and mania (labels she would never own). December 24 was my mother's favorite day of the year. The twenty-fifth came in a close second. The twenty-sixth ranked last out of the whole 365. We all kept our distance the day after Christmas, working stealthily to put away her museum-like collection of decorations without triggering her despair. Still, she'd say every year the same thing: *You know why December twenty-sixth is the saddest day of the year? It's as far from Christmas as a person can get.*

By day two, Mom couldn't take watching Matthew and me hold down the couch any longer. She demanded we eat. She stood at the top of the stairs that would almost claim her life a decade later, clutching her Chardonnay, her words part yell and part slur. "Who wants a sandwich?"

"We're good," I said. "Just watching TV."

She went away for a while, then came back drunker and angrier. Her pain had a texture as tangible as Matthew's, but tangled. She stumbled and bounced, a bumper car in the stairwell. I worried she might fall. She was a loose wire, her disease cannibalizing her maternal instincts in a heartbreaking act of destruction.

We hadn't always been like this. Mom was the kind of person who would tip a terrible server extra because she wanted to turn a stranger's bad day around. She was the kind of person who always kept a few extra presents under the tree so she could pencil in the name of whomever Matthew or I dragged home for the holiday on the fly. She was the person who hosted baby showers, and wedding showers, and brought food to any family suffering loss. She laughed more often than any other human I've known, and she had a rare talent for making even the strangest stranger feel at home.

One day I was ten and our house was filled more often than not with Mom and her friends drinking casually. Then I was fifteen and my own friends declared her open-minded and cool. I turned twenty and noticed she slurred and stumbled after an evening of drinking. Then I was twenty-seven and pulling her from the bushes outside my house at the end of the day when I officially became a Master of Writing.

One day we were one thing, and the next we were broken. Pain, fear, and a bad genetic draw can diminish anyone. Mom's fall into alcoholism was as slippery and insidious as Matthew's descent into drugs and depression.

To despair, I learned in my high school class on the Old Testament as literature, is to turn one's back on God, to have no faith or hope. Understand: Whatever god my mother had known had rendered her fatherless at fourteen, taken her first love in a car accident at fifteen, left her to raise her siblings while her mother drank and dated and stole her children's small inheritances, then found her pregnant at seventeen with a son who now rejected her and a husband whose strongest feelings for her no longer included love and a daughter who didn't say much one way or another.

She came again to top of the stairs, a leaning tower. "Do you want a sandwich?" she yelled. "Matthew, YOU NEED A SAND-WICH!"

Finally pushed to speak, his words cracked like gunfire in

still woods. "No," he said. "I don't. I don't want anything to eat. I don't want anything to drink. I don't want to talk." He used all his strength to be gentle with her, but he could not engage, could not be helped or touched. "It's okay, Mama. It's okay."

Mama, a word so different, I have learned, than *Mom* or *Mother.*

Her body relaxed as if Matthew had walked to the top of the stairs and wrapped his arms around her. *Mama.* The word unraveled her, leaving no defense against tears. She put herself to bed, holding on to her son's last gift: *Mama.*

That night, our parents went to dinner and left me to take Matthew shopping for work clothes. This was his Christmas gift. Presents in our youth had been extravagant: instruments, ice skates, electronics, skateboards, and such. As adults they were no less spendy: booze, books, gift certificates, always a Benjamin Franklin stuffed in each stocking. Since his split from Corey and the "incident" that no one described as a suicide attempt, he'd been demoted to a hundred-dollar limit on necessities at Walmart. To help *get him back on his feet.*

I used Mom's new Honda — a green CRV — to take the two of us that night. She had suddenly forbidden Matthew from using her car based on his years-old DUI, insisting I drive. The trip, however, was a good excuse for us to escape the crucible of the basement. My brother stared out the window, studying the familiar sights as I drove: a factory where he'd once worked, the meatpacking plant, our childhood church, both town graveyards, a house where he'd lived with a girlfriend. A cold rain darkened the asphalt and melted the snow berms.

Under the fluorescent lights of the big-box store, Matthew shopped mechanically, reading his size and throwing items into the cart still folded: three pairs of 501s, one pair of steel-toe boots, two flannels, two sets of long underwear, a canvas jacket, four T-shirts, and gloves. We paid, loaded up the car, and began the drive back. As we traversed the length of our hometown a second time, he loosened up.

"I came home to get sober," he said. "I came up here to not drink, and there's Mom, being drunk and crazy. She's going to drink herself to death. And Dad's a ghost. Won't mind his blood sugar and can't stop working."

We hadn't seen my father for more than a moment since I'd arrived. His presence felt opposite of Mom's. She filled up a room, her discontent a knife's edge. Dad appeared and disappeared — a gentle and soothing presence for a moment — then gone.

"I told Mom I'm not mad, but I don't want to talk about my marriage. I don't want to talk about your marriage. I don't want to talk about their marriage. I don't want to talk about anyone's marriage. I told her that."

I didn't want to talk about marriage either. It was too close for me to see clearly, like trying to estimate the size and shape of a mountain when you're standing on it. A year ago, I wanted to be part of a union like Mom and Dad, or Matthew and Corey. Now I worried Josh and I were susceptible to whatever disease infected my family.

Matthew looked out the window toward the flat, frosted landscape as Christmas lights flashed primary colors across his face. He took a deep breath, held it, and let go. "I just don't fucking know what to do. I don't fucking know, you know?"

I don't remember what I said, if anything at all. I only remember I was there, doing my imperfect best to care for him, and hoping beyond reason that my presence might in some small way tip the scales back into his favor.

Consider this: Matthew didn't die because you finally found your voice in that basement and said something so hard and true that he avoided you the rest of your lives, which he spent climbing on and off the wagon.

I woke the next morning to footsteps overhead and found Matthew loading up the Porsche. My parents must have been at work or out shopping, leaving me the sole witness to his departure. I stood silent as a doorknob, in my pajamas, as he walked up and down those stairs, draining the fridge of beer and the bar of liquor until the back end of the Porsche sank under the weight of the booze. His discomfort with his "new" car was clear as the color of the sky.

Though the Porsche had once been Dad's dream car — an eighties version of the Fiat he'd brought home when Mom was seventeen and nine months pregnant, it was a dated and glitchy beast by the time he gifted it to Matthew. While I'd always been a sucker for quirky imports of the five-door, four-cylinder variety, Dad's ideal vehicle had two doors, six cylinders, and a brisk zero-to-sixty acceleration time. Matthew was all-American. First he drove the Volaré, then a flat-faced Econoline van, and most recently the sixties Chevy. (No one mentioned what had become of it.) The Porsche was simply a means to an end for Matthew, a vehicle he would trade for the Ford in a few short weeks.

The only alcohol he left behind was the one drink neither of us could stomach: Mom's Chardonnay. When he saw her standing on the top of the stairs like that, I think he must have lost all hope that either of them might recover. He threw his backpack in the passenger's seat and gave me a single-armed hug. I wished for someone to tell him not to go, someone braver than me. But I choked on my own voice, losing him for good in the driveway of our childhood home, on New Year's Eve.

A ten-hour drive to Georgia lay ahead — he might still greet the new millennium with friends if he hurried. The top of his head bumped the roof as he crawled into the driver's seat. He fumbled the clutch, tires squealing as he pulled onto Lafayette Avenue and disappeared.

I never again saw him alive.

Part 4

FIFTEEN

Ford F-150

Georgia: 2000

I *WAKE ON OUR THIRD DAY* in Athens in a generic hotel. There's no Josh beside me, only my parents in a nearby
bed, and I close my eyes as I recall all over again that my brother
has died, and we've gathered here to close down his life. It's a vicious cycle: the forgetting, the waking, and the fresh wave of grief
that crashes over me as I remember. On this morning and many to
come, my hands press against my head as the picture of Matthew,
dead, returns. It's like cringing when you see someone stub a toe
— instinct over reason, and I lay there for a while, putting pressure
on my own head where the bullet entered his.

Examining the underside of my memories has left me more lost
than ever, with no conclusion but this: Matthew and I left Indiana, left each other, then he left me a dog and a truck. I have no
time for anything but the task at hand — getting Early from Georgia to Texas, across terrain I've never traveled, in a truck I've never
driven.

I arrive at the landfill by nine with a backpack and a gas card,
my face so red and swollen that I don't look like myself. Matthew's

friend and coworker Victor steps outside the office trailer and throws me a set of keys. Though my mother raised me to believe I have a hand-eye-coordination deficiency, I snatch them out of air like a character in *CHiPs* or *Magnum, P.I.*

Victor wears a black T-shirt, black jeans, and combat boots in the thick heat of the day. He's tall and gaunt, his pale skin so striking against his dark hair that the sun seems a danger to him. Matthew told me that Victor was once a member of an old punk band he admired. Victor looks more fit for the stage than the waking world.

"I hear she's yours." He runs a single finger along the Ford's silver trim.

"I guess."

"That's no ride for someone guessing."

"I have to get Early back is why." The dog, hearing his name, circles me a few times and stands sentry at my side. I stare at the Skyline trailer and daydream of moving in, keeping the dog and the truck, and shedding my Texas life like a snakeskin.

"You gotta own a truck like that." Victor makes eye contact to be sure I understand.

The sun glints off the cherry paint job. A Confederate flag license plate adorns the front bumper. Corrugated steel lines the bed — a toolbox behind the cab containing everything a roadside mechanic might need. He's right, about the truck. It more than shines. It dominates.

Once, while working one of my jobs at a coffee cart in a gas station parking lot in Missoula, I watched a Native American woman no bigger than me fix a truck like this. She opened the hood and perched on the edge of the engine compartment, unrolled a homemade cloth tool carrier, and went to work. She used her body weight as leverage to spring what stuck and mend it. She didn't buy a coffee or a water or a bag of chips or gas. She simply worked for an hour, washed the grease from her hands, and got back on the highway, her black hair whipping in the wind. She had something beyond wanderlust — a kind of confidence, a persistence. She had grit.

I stare down my brother's red truck, aware there's a fifty-fifty chance I might cry over a flat tire. But there's one thing before me not open for dispute: My brother's truck is a bona fide beaut.

"I called Matt's mechanic," Victor says. "He's on his way."

"What for?"

"Truck's touchy. Matt just had a bunch of work done. Carburetor problems. Wanna make sure it's all set 'fore you go. You can wait in there if you want." Victor gestures toward Matthew's trailer.

I turn my head in the opposite direction. If I go inside, I might not come out. I can't look at a single T-shirt without wanting to smell it, imagining him wearing it, his long spine now reduced to bone meal. I'm carrying my portion of him — about a quarter of the ash — in a wooden box in my backpack. We picked him up this morning, my father cradling his firstborn in a gold and black urn.

"I'll check out the truck." I say, jingling the keys to release Victor from duty.

"Well then. I'll be in there. In my office. You come in and have a smoke when you want." He is attractive in a Tom Petty kind of way. I would smile at him if I could still make my face do a trick like that.

The weight of the door comforts me as I open it — formidable, like the Volaré. The truck, after all, is a '79, only one year younger than our old Plymouth. I wonder if that drew Matthew to the truck, as it does me now.

The sun-heated cab smells like yellowed book pages and petrol.

Early jumps in and I follow, my hands resting on the wheel at ten and two. A black bra hangs from the rearview. I shut it in the glove compartment and crack a window. The after-market console between the passenger's side and the driver's side holds a collection of items covered with dust and sunlight. Amid the many cassette tapes are some half-packs of smokes, an assortment of colorful matchbooks, and a notepad from a Days Inn. The top sheet holds these words in my brother's handwriting: *Please find me where you know I need to be.* Dad will later identify this as a prayer, of sorts, from the Gary Zukav book *The Seat of the Soul,* which he'd given to Matthew in the past year.

The comfort and the irony of these words press into me — a dull edge. This is the closest thing to praying I've ever known my brother to do. A huge leap. A seed of hope and acceptance. But where *did* he need to be? Dead? I needed him here. We grew up — friends at last — and he checked out like he never loved us at all. *Please find me where you know I need to be.* Where did *I* need to be? At the dump? Ready to climb behind the wheel of my dead brother's truck with his glassy-eyed dingo riding shotgun?

> *Consider this: Your brother didn't die because the moment the bullet exited butterflies flew from his skull and the cicadas of northern Georgia erupted in three-part harmony, providing evidence (at last) that there are angels among us.*

I inspect the mix tapes in the console until a bleary-eyed fatigue overcomes me. The sight of Matthew's heavy-metal script on the tapes is too much. I stare through the windshield, the land before me brown and barren. The garbage cooks in the rising sun, and the smell of decomposition makes me think of his body.

In the office, Victor stares down a stack of stained and disheveled papers. He stands when he sees me and offers a spare chair. A giant boar's head hangs above us, dominating the small room — a third and omniscient presence. He watches me watch it.

"You want that? You can have it. I'll throw it in the truck right now. Come on. I will."

I thank him and decline, still staring.

"Think about it. Here, have a smoke." He lights one and passes it to me. His movements are fast and overly punctuated — the discomfort of a sober drunk or a user.

I do want the boar's head, but I would never say so. It belongs with Victor, something to keep him company in Matthew's absence. They worked days together, overseeing the inmates.

"You want his record collection? I'll have it shipped. I will."

The records. I spent an hour sifting through them in the trailer, touching each one with the care and reverence some might save for the Bible. It was an epic collection, starting with the records my mother gathered as a teen (the "the" bands: the Beatles, the Beach Boys, the Turtles, the Monkees). Those snowballed into my parents' joint vinyl purchases: everything from Janis Joplin to Jackson Browne and Elton John. And finally my brother's contributions made up the bulk of the archive — early punk, metal, and more recent alt country finds. He even had my old David Bowie, the *Let's Dance* album he tricked me into buying. It never occurred to me to claim his vinyl.

"Okay," I said. "The records would be great."

Victor pauses for a moment. "Great. I'll send them. That's something I can do." He drums his desk with a pencil and smiles.

Something I can do. That's the whole of it. There is nothing to be done. Matthew is dead. But all anyone wants to do is fix it, or fix something. The boar's eyes fix on the window, unchanged by the tides of the finite world.

"I know you gotta drive and all, but I think you should have a taste of this." Victor ducks underneath his desk and surfaces with two paper cups. "Matt would want you to. He was making this on the sly with one of the inmates. We was gonna let them drink some when it was done." He whispers the part about giving the inmates booze.

I take a sniff and a peek. There's some fruit pulp floating in what looks like vodka with a dash of grenadine.

"Strawberry wine. Not bad, huh?" Victor kicks his combat boots up on the desk and starts humming a song as he sips. "I took it out of his place the night he died. Because I knew your family and the cops would come. Thought you all might throw it out." His face wrinkles with sudden concern, as if he only now realizes I might think him a thief. "I hope you don't mind."

"No. I'm glad you saved it. It's good."

He relaxes again. "It coulda set a while longer, but I plan to give the inmates a shot today, when I tell them about Matt. They loved him, you know. We all —" His voice breaks and he shrugs, bereft. We give up talking and blow smoke in arcs until it fills the room, drifts through the window, and out into the day.

The mechanic arrives, adjusts a few things, and warns me about driving too hard in the heat. He tells me three times to check the oil at every stop. It is clear to all of us that the business of me piloting this two-ton truck is questionable at best. Making off with my brother's prized possessions (the truck and the dog) is not the coup I imagined when we were kids. It is, in fact, pure necessity at this point. His death robbed all he loved of value. Me included.

It's noon by the time the mechanic green-lights the journey. I buckle myself in, the engine running already. Victor salutes me, statuesque in my rearview, as the vacant Skyline and the mountains of garbage fall away. The truck drives like a weapon on wheels. I aim south, toward Atlanta, the junction that will turn us west to Texas, a state where I don't yet belong.

As I pull onto the highway I think about how I am in this moment a resident of nowhere. I think about how just yesterday, mere miles from here, strangers loaded my brother's body into an incinerator, stripped down to tattoos. Flames enveloped him, burning away flesh, the face, the organs — reducing him irrevocably to a twenty-pound pile of ash. I think about how my father took that urn in his arms and looked up at us this morning, astonished. *He's the weight of a baby again,* he said.

One of Matthew's mix tapes catches my eye. He's written on the spine a title of his own creation: *It Ain't Fun No More.*

He'd left a tape instead of a note. I slide it into the stereo and rewind to the start of the A side. The first song guts me. Trying to see the road through my tears is like driving through a car wash.

The song is too sentimental for Matthew. The band too popular. But there's no mistaking his message: *Tattoos and memories and dead skin on trial / For what it's worth it was worth all the while . . .*

The yellow and white lines of the highway guide me. The margin of error no longer scares me. I hold steady at sixty-five. The dog pants, eyes on the horizon.

It Ain't Fun No More.

Each mile takes me farther and farther from the remnants of a brother. Each mile a wound, an effort, and a chance.

In the late afternoon I stop for gas in Alabama, a state I've never visited. My bones vibrate with fatigue. The only thing steadying me is the hum of tires on pavement. I pull up to the pump and realize I have no idea where the gas tank lives on the truck. I put it in park, walk the perimeter until I find the gas cap, then make a six-point turn to get to the pump. My ineptitude draws sideways stares. The station is on the outskirts of Birmingham and it's busy, most of the customers black. At a time when I want most to be invisible, I've become painfully conspicuous. This truck is a liability, a sentence, a shoe waiting to drop.

I stand with Early's leash in hand, my black tank-top exposing a sliver of belly above the waistline of my thrift-store Wranglers. I'm sporting black Converse and horn-rimmed glasses. My dark hair stands short and wild after three days of inattention and the open-windowed drive. One of Matthew's friends told me I looked like Joan Jett, but I feel more like Peter Pan: a lost child in need of friends. I am, more accurately, a petite woman with a half-sleeve tattoo, an overweight blue heeler, and a hot rod truck bearing the Confederate flag on the front plate. A damsel in distress. Privileged. A problem. I pull into a parking spot to walk Early Times. He prances through the hot, damp grass, licks a fast food wrapper, and pisses on a signpost. He minds me better than my own dogs.

I can handle driving, but walking disorients me. It feels like stepping off a boat after a week at sea. I haven't much eaten since the few bites of the bad salmon dinner back in San Marcos, and I've got no sunglasses to shield me from the sun holding steady in the blank blue sky.

Back in the truck, I review the route, forming a mantra out of the highway numbers I must remember: *85 to 65 to 10.* I turn the key. The engine catches and dies. I try again. Nothing. Again. No luck. I smell gas, and in my right mind I might know it is flooded. But logic vanishes, leaving my emotions in control. I've never driven a vehicle with a carburetor before. I stand outside that truck, hood up, and plead for help with my eyes. A small black man in his sixties glances in my direction while putting oil in his truck. Our eyes connect for the briefest moment. He walks over, reluctant, like I'm dangerous.

"It won't start."

"It's done flooded." He takes a look at the carburetor.

"It's my brother's truck. He died on Sunday. I don't know anything about it."

The man looks around, nervous. "Give it twenty minutes. Start it up, then drive yourself straight home."

Home. It is a word without connection.

"I'm going to Texas."

"You'll be okay. Just start it up and drive. Don't be standing 'round here. Understand?"

"Yes," I say as he walks away. "Thank you."

I smoke a cigarette in the cab of the truck, noticing the man slowly checking his tire pressure and air filter. After a bit, he shoots me a look to signal it's time. I turn the key. Smoke comes out the back — gas burning off. In the rearview, I see the man watch over my departure like some kind of roadside angel, his hands in the pockets of his polyester slacks — the same Lee Riders my Papaw wears.

A decade later, I make email contact with Corey on a whim. Though I won't say the words, an apology is what I'm after — some proof that she knows the devastation she triggered in our lives. What she says to me is this (and this alone): *Missy, I believe there are angels in this world masquerading as humans. Matthew was one of them.*

I understand then that the reparations I am after can't be exacted from her. I want her to tell me how guilty she feels, how the way she introduced Matthew to her world then abandoned him was wrong, how she is a garbage human who never deserved a moment of my brother's attention. I want her to say her life is ruined and she spends every day haunted and hollow, but wanting anything from her is like knocking on the door of an empty house, a feeling I suspect my brother knew well.

We never speak or write or see each other again.

Consider this: Your brother didn't die, because he said yes to art school, eventually moving west instead of south, where he designed album covers and never lived in a trailer or drank all the booze or picked up the Glock.

The drive across the south in Matthew's truck begins to feel like a fatigue-induced acid trip without end. A couple hours past the gas station in Alabama, I start passing out — an experience that feels distinctly different from nodding off. My vision simply dissolves into television fuzz while my eyes stay open. I slap myself awake until my cheeks turn red from abuse.

I check in to a hotel at four in the afternoon, order a pizza I can't stomach, and fall asleep with Early at my feet. We hit the road around three the next morning, hoping to clock some miles before the day heats up. At one point, I change lanes and nearly take out a station wagon. The truck has blind spots. Around midday, I attempt a nap in a rest stop in Louisiana, but the sun is too fierce for rest.

There is no way around it — I roll into Houston at rush hour on a Wednesday and spend two long hours in traffic, afraid both the truck and dog might overheat. I roll a cold water bottle on Early's belly and let him drink from an open Big Gulp cup on the console. It's well over one hundred. I'm braless and wearing my smallest shorts, but even driving naked wouldn't bring relief.

Near nightfall, I bring the truck to a stop in our San Marcos driveway. Early charges into the house and instigates a three-way dogfight. Josh and I yell and pull and bribe until the dogs are safely exiled to the backyard. They growl and stare, sorting out the new pack dynamics.

"You brought Early," Josh says, raising his eyebrows in that *what the fuck* kind of way he's so good at.

In the chaos of the past few days, I overlooked telling him. Didn't even think to ask. The addition of Early means we have three dogs — about two hundred pounds of combined canine weight — living in a two-bedroom bungalow hemmed in by heat and traffic in a town we don't yet know and don't much like.

"No one would take him." I shrug my shoulders. "I didn't know what to do."

Josh runs a hand over his eyes and sighs.

Our friend Neil finishes off a PBR and assesses the situation. "Wanna go see some music in Austin?"

"When?" I say.

"Like, right now?"

There is nothing else I'd rather do than keep moving and start drinking. Neil and I crack road beers, thrilled that open containers are legal in Texas for passengers. The three of us pile into the truck — Josh driving, me in the middle, Neil riding shotgun. Lights make trails in the night like sparklers on the Fourth of July. I let my vision go blurry the way I used to in the Volaré, back in Indiana, when we were young and still alive.

SIXTEEN

Breakdown

Texas: August 2000

*N*OT LONG AFTER MY RETURN from Georgia, I'm piloting Matthew's two-ton behemoth solo on an access
road when the horn goes off — again. *Honk honk. Honk honk honk
HONK*. It's rush hour in San Marcos, the traffic thick and aggressive in a way I never experienced in Montana. My hand aches as
I grip the wheel, knuckles scraped raw from abusing a live oak in
the KFC parking lot minutes ago. I'd pulled over when the horn
first went off, thinking I could fix this thing — one simple thing —
but I can't. Things are broken — are breaking. Heat waves ema-
nate from the cherry hood, distorting my view of the road. I use
my good hand to offer other drivers my best drowning-not-wav-
ing gesture while silently praying to Matthew: *Please make it stop
so I don't get the shit beat out of me.* I turn on to the street that
leads to our house. There's a park on one side, the best Mexican
restaurant in town on the other, and the river nearby. A few teenage girls in swimsuits walk leisurely in front of me. I slow down
for them, but the horn won't stop. *Honk honk HONK.* They look
up, surprised to see me instead of a man in the driver's seat. They
stop in the road, speaking in Spanish, confused.

"I AM SO SORRY," I yell. "THE HORN IS BUSTED!"

I don't know if they understand me, but they move on, whispering and laughing as they go.

Two blocks later I coast to a stop in our driveway, cut the engine, and listen to the heat tick out of her. It's egg-cooking hot. 111 degrees, I later learn on the nightly news. My body is ungrounded, short-circuiting everything I touch.

That night, at the first good bar we've found in San Marcos — a place called the Showdown — I ask around for something I've never needed: a repair shop that handles domestics. Over a few drinks, I recount my experience for Josh and Neil. Their laughter is a consolation prize, but the incident remains unsettling. The only way I get my feet on the ground each morning is by believing Matthew is with me, somehow, protecting me in a way he rarely did when he was alive. I want the truck to feel like a sacred place where my brother's ghost rides shotgun. It drives instead like a speeding corpse, a boat ride to Hades — the truck version of Stephen King's Christine.

During those first few weeks back, Early growls at Josh when he comes to bed. Josh yells for me to calm Earl so he can turn in without fearing attack by a junkyard dog. I begin calling Early Earl for the same reasons I insisted people call me Melissa instead of Missy around the time I started middle school. *Earl* is six years old. *Earl* has been through some things. *Early* was just a dog.

Meanwhile, the heat hangs on to triple digits well into September, something I never dreamed possible. The dogs pace and whine, unsatisfied with short, hot walks and river swims. I crank the air, knit on the couch, and watch them curl and uncurl in their sleep, chronically uncomfortable.

Josh suffers his own grief — over leaving his hometown, searching for random jobs, grieving his brother-in-law, gaining a third dog, and, in ways, losing his brand-new wife. While sadness is my response to what's happened, anger is his. Texas burned the light right out of him. Still, he tries to cheer me up with a drive to San Antonio. I buy a stuffed armadillo at a curio shop because of a John Irving book my mother and I love: *A Prayer for Owen Meany.* Maybe the armadillo will guide me, I think, as I cradle the dead animal, run my fingers over its hide. We wander over to the Alamo and search for the spot where Ozzy Osbourne is rumored to have urinated. Even that can't wring from me a simple smile.

I find the door in my head that I use to escape sticky situations, and I hole up there, burrowing so deep that the only person who can find me is Matthew. In some ways I feel closer to him than ever. While the rest of the world averts their eyes in hopes that I won't say too much about my "sudden loss," my grief does not scare him.

In September I begin buying my own packs of smokes again, give up running, trade a half-decade of vegetarianism for Texas barbecue, and start graduate school at the university on the hill that looms above downtown. There is no thought behind these changes. The part of me that cared to take care of myself no longer lives here. The part that believed in ambition, hard work, and progress. Instead, I pass days satisfying my appetites and searching out pressure for my wounds.

The only dreams I dream any longer involve Matthew, our past, or fleeing the state in my Volkswagen van, aimed toward the hills of Brown County — the place I remember us happiest. Dad tells me that Betty and Don are moving to Florida and selling the A-frame he helped them build. I can't remember the last time I saw it — the mid-eighties, perhaps? I remember spending a week there with Aunt Lisa's daughter Emily. She was five, which puts me around ten. Betty accused me of using her makeup without asking. I hadn't, but I blushed and nodded, accepting the blame for my young cousin's actions — so prone I am to guilt that I'll adopt it from others. Dad says the house has fallen into disrepair. He says it's probably a teardown by now, but I suspect this is only to discourage my interest. If I had any money, I'd buy it and retreat there solo, become a hill person with nothing to my name but a van and a truck and acres of quiet.

My life feels like roadkill, a mess beyond fixing, only my brain won't stop thinking any more than I could talk my heart out of beating. I live because my body does, a black hole incarnate.

Afternoons I walk partway home from classes, stop for a drink or five at the Showdown, then stumble on in the dark, chasing an armadillo or flushing out a nutria if the urge to dunk my feet in the river strikes. My sadness isn't fiery like my mother's or my brother's. It falls over me like a wet wool blanket. I wander through days dislocated — searching for the *when, why,* and *how* of my being. I don't have to search far and wide for Jägermeister shots, Shiner Bock pints, Cape Cods, or margaritas. Is this how Matthew felt when he stopped wanting anything, or knew what he wanted would kill him?

We make friends. At the bar. At school. Neil remains our steady. The same calm that angered me the night of Matthew's death renders him invaluable afterward. He finds an old army barracks to live in, the cinderblock walls a confirmation of what he believes life has to offer — a cheap rental that won't cost a grad student his beer money.

The three of us soon meet Tony Chapa, a Mexican American military veteran and PhD student from San Antonio. He has an infectious smile and spends evenings at the Showdown with us. One night, I tell him Matthew's story from beginning to end — how we grew up, grew apart, grew close, then *bam* — gone. Tony's face droops like a tent with a broken pole.

"I'm sorry if I said something wrong."

He takes a swig of beer and wipes his brow. "It's hard to hear, is all. And there's nothing I can do to make it better, Mel. It's just plain sad."

His gift of a nickname makes us instant friends, but I'm left to process a secondary loss: the stories I loved best, the stories that used to make people laugh, now make them cringe. Without Matthew stories, I have little to say, and less to write.

Matthew was the best part of my life, and he didn't wanted to live. Why should I?

Consider this: You went to grad school in Iowa instead of Texas and came to hate corn stalks and snow instead of fire ants and humidity. To distract yourself, you ran off with a writer fifteen years your elder and spent the rest of your life revolving around his voice.

A short while later, Chapa (as we call him) stops by the house and asks to borrow my van to help him move from one apartment to another. This van has taken me through the Midwest to the Rocky Mountains, all the way to the West Coast, through desert, to San Francisco and back. It housed me through brief stretches of homelessness and nights spent in concert parking lots, my brain a pair of Reagan-era eggs in a frying pan. This van I'd sewn curtains for, made a bed in, and driven over the icy roads of the Olympic peninsula and through Montana blizzards before sun-up. This van transported Josh's band equipment for his gigs and brought home two of my three dogs. This van is my ride, my freedom, my middle finger to the world of modern jellybean cars made out of fiberglass, built to expire. This van I've owned for eight years — longer than any car in my life.

But it is a Tuesday and my brother is two weeks dead and I am home alone, day-drinking in our air-conditioned bungalow. I throw Chapa the keys like they are nothing.

"Check the oil and watch the engine temp, okay?"

"Thanks, Mel." Chapa flashes me a peace sign and his everlasting smile.

Outside, the *tick-tick-tick* of the waterboxer engine fades as he drives away. The house falls silent, and I fall back into the house. Aside from the constant hum of the strained AC unit, the groans and sighs of the dogs, or the click of their overgrown nails on hardwood, my thoughts are my soundtrack. I crack another beer, sit at my desk in my office, and let my gaze fall to the baseboards.

I think about my brother's head a lot. While I was relieved it remained more or less intact, I wonder what Randy saw when he came back to the trailer and found Matthew's body bleeding, soul fleeing. He was face-up, Randy said. I picture a quickly spreading pool of blood around him, dark red on white linoleum.

I dream myself into the scenario: I rush in to find him, my keys jingling as they hit the floor. I fall to my knees, landing in blood and grab his chin, turn his face toward mine so I can look directly in his eyes. Though his gaze is fixed, I check his pulse and find the heart's faint *beat beat beat*. I jump up, almost slipping in the blood, and call 911. Next to him again, the world is too quiet. I examine the entry wound behind his right ear, a black hole the size of a quarter. Then I return him face-up and we wait for the sirens.

This is where the daydream replays over and over. What did the exit wound look like? A hole the size of a silver dollar from his childhood coin collection, maybe? Were there shards of skull? Bits of scalp and hair? Could I, if I tried, see a bit of his brain?

It's morbid, I know, like when Matthew, as a kid, dug up the Ball jar that held his dead pet. Though he had loved his hamster, Rocky Chinese, decay fascinated him. Dad got worried after he found Matthew sleeping with tiny, jarred corpse — by then nothing but tufts of fur clinging to toothpick bones.

I don't talk about my daydreams, but my silence doesn't stop them. Time passes, my mind cast back to scenes past and imagined. The farther I go, the less I come back. I become a soul haunt-ing a body, a ghost in search of a ghost.

The phone rings in the here and now — the one filled with beer and visions and restless dogs. It is Tony.

"Melissa. Man, I'm sorry, but your van won't start."

"What do you mean it won't start?" My van has never, in the past eight years, refused to start (save for that one subzero time at the Lariat Hotel in Wyoming when water froze in the gas line).

"It's dead."

"Dead?"

"I got a ride from a friend with a truck, so I'm good. It's in the taco shop parking lot near your place. You need a ride?"

"No thanks."

"Sorry, Mel. I owe you a beer. Keys are in the visor."

I slip on flip-flops and walk the blocks through late-day sun to the taco joint. I imagine Chapa eating in the stalled-out van, wait-ing for his friend to come, then abandoning my ride like she's just some thing. I climb behind the wheel and flip down the visor. The keys fall into my lap.

Hey, I whisper to her, *I'm here.*

I apologize for pimping her out, hoping we can come to some sort of agreement. I press the clutch and brake and turn the key. Nothing. I try a few more times, but she gives not even the whirl of the starter. The lights and gauges work, so it isn't the battery. It's the worst kind of Volkswagen problem — an electrical gremlin. This is pretty far from okay, but I am ghost drunk and can't muster enough feeling to spark a proper reaction.

There's a phone booth in the parking lot. It must be 100 inside. I call AAA for a tow, then flip through the yellow pages, finding only one import garage listed — a place called Lester's. The name makes me laugh out loud. While I had been partial in my youth to sending away for brochures and catalogues using faux movie star names, Matthew's skateboarding magazines arrived addressed to his own alter egos, most often Tammy Pon and Mo Lester. I laugh until my stomach hurts, drain my beer in a single pull, cry until my head throbs, and compose myself as the AAA truck arrives.

The driver approaches the van with the nonchalance of someone for whom roadside emergencies are routine. He talks while glancing from the van to his clipboard, his voice short and rough.

"This your van?"

"Yes."

"Rear-wheel drive?"

"Yes."

"Where to?"

"Lester's."

"Got your card?"

"Sure." I hand over proof of membership, and he registers the wreckage of my face, his expression changing from locked to alarmed. I no longer think to dry my eyes.

"Ma'am. You okay?"

"Oh, sure." I find his shift toward humanity sweet, this southern tendency to ma'am people awkward, and his question ridiculous. *Okay?* No, I'm not okay.

He rigs up the van's rear wheel, lifts her back end, and drives down the road, my eyes on her headlights until she's out of sight.

But you'll be okay! I want to tell her.

I head toward the river to watch the ebb and flow with nothing on my person — no bag, keys, or beer — just a pair of cheap flip-flops and thrift-store clothes.

I don't know why I want to see Matthew's exit wound, but I do. Death had been his last performance, and we'd missed it. Since he didn't stick around to tell us the tale, I can't help but write it over and over in my head, down to the panting of Early as he lay beside him, a bullet hole in the ceiling, and blood glistening dark and shiny as Mom's date-night nail polish.

Matthew spent his last years resenting others for reducing him to a stereotype, though with each tattoo and new substance he became the more of the thing he loathed. I think he liked my stories because they humanized him. I do this now, for myself, replaying that final day so that I might understand how he felt, how death opened him up, blowing a vent in his head to let all those shark dreams out.

Consider this: Your brother survived the Glock shot but sustained a brain injury that left him wheelchair-bound, unable to speak for the rest of his surprisingly long life.

After a few weeks hunting for jobs, Josh begins full-time training to become a guard at a corrections facility about twenty miles up the interstate in Kyle, Texas. I assure him it will be a character-building stopgap, a funny story to retell over drinks one day. But we both know he is signing on to be an oppressor, like the guard in *Cool Hand Luke* with the mirrored sunglasses. We both know Matthew is the Paul Newman of that equation, even when he became a prison guard in his last year so he could oversee the inmates at the landfill. The new job is a sore spot we avoid, neither of us wanting to admit we are going over to the dark side in order to pay the bills. Our life seems a house of mirrors, an image distorted by heat.

As his job training begins, Josh leaves the house five days a week, giving me space. I covet solitude the way Matthew once coveted Jim Beam. I sink into the hours, sifting through old mix tapes from Matthew to me, from me to him, from high school friends and college loves. I catalogue the artifacts I took from his trailer: photo albums, half-written poems, gun receipts (a couple shotguns, the Glock, a Winchester rifle, and sale ads for AK-47s), to-do lists even (*Tuesday: pay loan, Blockbuster, dog chews, grocery, Lotto ticket, tattoo Tim, clean gun*).

I pass nights sitting in the dark on the couch and find that if I look straight ahead, letting my eyes fix and shifting my awareness to my peripheral vision, Matthew materializes next to me. Objects dead center dissolve into television fuzz. The air begins to vibrate the way it did when I was young and traveled without my body because no one had told me not to. Now my brother sits beside me in his old green hoodie, Levi's, and work boots. He gazes toward the floor, shy with shame, the way he was in our parents' basement, the last time I saw him in his body.

Every time he appears it destroys me. My mind is already a too-short film reel set on repeat. When he shows up like that, grief infects me — a physical illness.

I can never tell how much time I spend rebuilding the architecture of his face, or replaying his soft, low voice in my head. I encourage every detail, afraid to un-remember, because when those images go, I'll be left alone again — my body no more than an abandoned house on some bypassed blue highway.

Consider this: Your brother downed twenty-seven Jell-O shots one Sunday in Georgia, blasted a bullet through his skull, and it was no one's fault but his.

SEVENTEEN

Gremlins

Texas: 2000

O N A MONDAY AFTERNOON I muster the energy to drive the truck over to a shop called Frank's. I have no idea if the place is any good, but it is close to the house. With Josh driving the Honda to prison five days a week and the van lost to Lester's, I'll have to walk home after I hand over the keys. I take mostly vacant neighborhood streets where the occasional horn honk causes no commotion.

The lobby of Frank's sports a Nascar theme, the floor black and white like a checkered flag. Pictures of famous drivers hang on the walls. Two workers speak Spanish to each other. They wear work shirts with those name patches Matthew loved so much. The place is larger and more professional than I expected. There is a garage with four or five lifts and a parking area surrounded by an eight-foot chainlink fence. A man at the desk takes my information.

"I called about the horn going off on my truck." I gesture out the window toward the Ford glowing in the midday sun.

"That is a beautiful truck." He gives us both a once-over, trying to figure out the pairing.

"It was my brother's."

"I see." He smiles, sympathetic. "We'll take care of it."

I set the keys on the counter and fill out a paper or two. The mechanic and I regard for a moment Matthew's keychain: a sterling skeleton on its knees, arms overhead in protection from some imminent and unseen blow. An effigy.

"You need a ride, ma'am?"

"No thanks. I can walk."

He waits until I walk away to touch the keys, out of respect or fear of contagion, I can't know.

At home, the answering machine blinks its red eye. I hit play.

This is Lester from Lester's Automotive. Just wanted you to know I've had your van towed to Pierre's. I can give you the address. Pierre's great with imports. He'll figure out what's wrong.

For the first time since before I bought the Turd, I am without wheels of my own. My independence rests in the hands of Lester, Frank, and now some guy named Pierre — a thing I promised myself I'd never again let happen after that trip to Alaska. A stranger in a land full of unfamiliar sights, smells, and customs, I am paralyzed by grief and busted-up cars. My husband is running on empty as well, up at four each morning to drive himself to prison for training. I can find no way around our new grown-up existence, no vehicle even to carry me off, under the night light of those famous Texas stars.

> Consider this: Your brother didn't die but kicked the junk, got a divorce, and become a functional alcoholic. Through dedication and indoctrination, he worked his way up to middle management at an auto parts franchise, where he was, more often than not, employee of the month.

Sleep becomes respite. In dreams I rummage through shapeshifting houses, attempting to make each my own until some mission calls me back to the road, where I wander (always on foot), find another house, and begin brushing decades of dust from still-made beds, telephone tables, and footlockers filled with strangers' photos. I sleep ten hours a night, mostly on the couch, Josh gone long before the pacing dogs and unstoppable light wake me.

I'm at school by noon most days. The routine soothes me with its mix of newness and structure. In order to earn a small income, I've taken a position as a teaching assistant in a lecture class on early American literature. I sit to the side of the stage and click through PowerPoint slides while a teacher my father's age reads from notes handwritten on yellow paper. The professor is, understandably, a bit of a Luddite. His slides are glitchy, and neither of us can figure out how to go backwards without quitting the whole program, re-starting the computer, and forwarding through to the right slide. Every time one of our two hundred students asks to go back to the previous slide, it takes five minutes for me to reboot and shuffle to some note about humor and race in early Mark Twain.

My writing classes are the reason we came to Texas in the first place. They provide an oasis from the heat and grief that shape my days, but everything I write is stillborn. Without stories of Mat-thew, my creative bank is in the red. Though I spend every mo-ment with him on my mind, I can no longer write about him. Never does it occur to me that I have stories of my own worth telling.

I search the yellow pages for Pierre's shop but find no listing. I wait a week to take further action because of poverty and inertia, though during that week I do make time to examine every photo from my childhood, make four mix tapes of songs that remind me of Matthew, and replay the day of my brother's death a hundred times — easy.

The next week, I call Lester. "I had my 'eighty-four Vanagon towed to you, and you had it towed to Pierre's, but I can't find a number for Pierre."

"Oh, sure. Just head up Ranch Road twelve like you're going to Wimberley. Turn at the drive about five miles out of town where you see all the foreign cars. That's him."

"But what's his number? What's the name of his shop?"

Lester laughs, privy to an inside joke. "Pierre don't have a phone. You just gotta find him. He's the only import guy south of Austin. You can go up to Austin, but they'll take your whole paycheck."

"I don't have a paycheck."

"Then you better talk to Pierre, darlin'. You got some kind of electrical thing going on. Them are two things I don't do: Volkswagens and electrical."

"You must love Saabs."

Lester laughs again, and my spirits rise over a well-delivered car joke. It makes me feel, for a moment, like an insider.

On one of Josh's days off, I take the Honda to search for Pierre's place. Josh is six weeks into his eight-week training, which means he will soon become a certified prison guard. The closer he comes to that day, the less he sleeps, the more we drink, and the darker the circles grow under his deep-set eyes. With no way to fix what ails him, I shy away from his unhappiness the same way people avoid my rampant and regular tears. My distance enrages him: He needs my help, my love, my guidance, but my cup is empty. I can't take care of myself or the van or the truck. I sure as hell can't begin to mend what's plaguing him. I fall into an emotional hibernation, inventing a future in which I leave for parts unknown. Though I don't understand these urges, the outcome is a form of self-inflicted manslaughter: the annihilation of my old self, the one who'd rather die than outlive her older brother. His death makes change seem so possible, like I could step out of my old life and into a new one with no more consideration than I'd give a change of clothes.

My trip into the Hill Country in search of a Frenchman and a gathering of foreign cars brings me nearly to hives. I smoke and drive, half hoping to miss the place and have AAA tow the van up to Austin the next day — all so I won't have to deal with the social anxiety of meeting a stranger. Before I can talk myself out of this adventure, I spot a sprinkling of foreign cars on the right side of the road. First, an early-eighties Mercedes wagon surrounded by tall, unbent grass. A quarter-mile later, a trio of MGs — parts cars, from the unkempt look of them. Finally, a driveway cutting through a field scattered with cars.

I steer down the dirt two-track, through a thicket of cedars, then pause for a moment to wait out a chicken in my path.

"Keep driving! They will move!"

I hear the voice but can't locate the source. Ahead I spy the core of this complex: a small wooden house with a porch and a barn a stone's throw away. The barn looks weathered by years, the house made more recently out of old materials. The work of an environmentalist.

"It's okay — keep going!"

I take my foot off the brake and let the Honda — an automatic — crawl toward the compound. A small man stands in the doorway to the barn, holding a wrench and regarding me like an unexpected package.

There is no clear place to park, only dirt with patches of grass and tumbleweeds. "This okay?"

"Oh, sure. You know. Anywhere."

The man raises his leather hat and smooths back shaggy brown hair. He has the kind of permanent tan that comes from years spent working in the sun. The sleeves of his faded button-down roll to the elbows, complemented by brown work pants, brown boots, a brown belt, and brown eyes. He is almost camouflaged against the brown barn and landscape. This man and place, I think, are my middle name in motion.

The vehicles offer the only color — a red Beamer, a yellow Fiat, an orange Peugeot — but layers of dirt mute their vibrant shades. This is an automotive dust bowl — a private depression from which it's hard to believe any engine might emerge revived, but it is peaceful, too. A place to retreat, to surrender. Disappear.

I know two things instantly: that this is Pierre, and that I belong in this automotive sanctuary more than I belong anywhere. In a heartbeat I fantasize about folding down the rear seat in my van, making up the bed, and setting up camp without telling the world where I have gone.

I step out of the Honda and introduce myself. Pierre is somewhere in his forties and not much taller or wider than me.

"Follow me," he says. We walk behind the barn where the van rests. I have missed her. Water stings my eyes for an instant before evaporating in the persistent heat wave.

"This is your van?" Pierre comes close but does not touch her.

"That's her." The sight of those round headlights calms me.

"What a piece of shit," he says.

The word *shit* sounds like *sheet* in his heavy accent. I am stunned but smiling. This small Frenchman is talking smack about my ride. I reach for my smokes.

"Away with that junk."

For a second, I think he's talking about the van. Then he pulls a pouch of tobacco from his shirt pocket and rolls two cigarettes. "Those are nothing but chemicals. Poison. You are young and beautiful. You try this." Pierre lights both smokes at once.

He called me beautiful.

"So you took a look at the van?"

My question seems to bore Pierre. He glances sideways at me, head aimed toward a gathering of Volkswagens segregated behind the barn. My van blends into the surroundings, though the coat of dust forming on her is thin compared to the accumulation on the three Beetles, two Squarebacks, one Fox, and a sweet Rabbit truck. He shrugs.

"You know. Not yet. But I will sniff around. These things are complicated."

His accent bends the word *sniff* into *sneef*. My van is a piece of *sheet*. Pierre is going to *sneef* around.

I wait for him to ask what went wrong so I can tell the story of the breakdown, but he doesn't. Matthew's death has become a lesson in the things people don't ask.

"She's always been reliable —" I say.

Pierre laughs while blowing smoke out of his nose. "She? It is a van. This van does not look reliable to me. It doesn't even start."

I stand in silence, considering the facts. My van's future is uncertain at best, but I decide to trust Pierre. After all, I am low on funds and in no hurry.

"Did you build your house?"

"I move here from France two decades ago. I followed a woman." He notices my wedding ring, lifts my hand. "Why are you married so young? You can't be twenty."

"Almost twenty-six."

"The woman left me, but I stayed. I bought this land. The barn was here, but the old house I could not save. I leveled it and built this."

The porch wraps around two sides of the house. Sheets of galvanized steel serve as a roof, the siding a collection of graying wood, the windows mismatched. A few chickens peck around the fringes of this ragged loveliness.

Pierre talks for two hours, about the best years for Mercedes, about the way cars were once built to last, about obese Americans and overconsumption, about living off the grid — hydroelectric energy, solar power, composting toilets. It is nice to listen to someone talk, someone who doesn't know much of anything about me, or what I've lost.

"I better get going," I say.

Pierre raises an eyebrow and nods.

"When should I come back? I mean, when do you think you can take a look?"

He draws in a breath and stares toward the cluster of German outcasts. "I'll sneef around. You come back next week. Yes?"

"Yes."

I drive away slowly, pausing here and there to check out the cars. I love them, but they worry me too — all of them stranded, deteriorating. Peaceful but without purpose, if such a thing is possible. As I turn onto the highway, a Dylan lyric Matthew loved comes to mind: *Those not busy being born are busy dying.*

Consider this: Josh refused to move to Texas so you went alone, his fresh hurt the missing ingredient needed to push his garage band on to a mediocre level of success. Your brother came to visit, consoling you with cold drinks and loud shows. He ended up keeping you company for years.

Josh quits the prison gig during his final week of training.

"The boss-man gave me a speech about how much money they invested in my training, how I owe it to them to work for at least a year."

We stand in the kitchen drinking beers that break a sweat even with the air on full blast. We are inching toward October — closing in on two months past Matthew's expiration — and the highs still graze the hundreds most days.

"You don't owe them shit." I put my hand on his hand.

He needs a break. He needs to feel useful, valuable. I need an open-ended vacation, car keys, a map, and some cash. Instead, we have three dogs, a small house, and each other.

"I get my first paycheck in a week," I tell him. "We'll be okay."

"I'll find something."

"I know."

What he finds next is a better shitty job at a sports news website based out of Austin. He works from four in the morning until noon, which means he's up by three to commute. His already fragile sleep patterns continue to deteriorate. Our love could still become the kind where we can lean on each other, if only I could keep myself from leaning away.

Some nights I stay up searching the Internet for clues to the Vanagon's silent treatment. *Is it the battery? Spark plugs? Fuel injectors? The starter? Alternator?* The idea that I could fix a Volkswagen is ridiculous, but it's something to focus on other than Matthew, who is beyond repair. I Google all leads and end up as confused and frustrated as Earl in one of his daily tail-chasing fits.

Some nights I squander listening to music and studying maps. On one such night, I'm so deaf with headphones on and a map of the States spread before me that Josh's touch makes me jump.

"Oh fuck," I say. "Fuck. You scared the fuck out of me."

"Sorry. But what are you doing up? With that map?"

I look down at the states, the highways, the stars of cities, embarrassed. It's like he's busted me, but for what we won't say.

"Just looking," I tell him — a lie. Part of me has left already while part of me remains, and I want desperately to join myself.

This need to flee isn't a choice. It came threaded in my DNA as far as I can tell. For me, *move* is to *pain* as *pressure* is to *wound*.

I was three the first time I got stung by a bee and I ran into the house screaming. Mom ran after me, terrified by the sound of me hurt. I remember it — how I ran into my parents' bedroom and jogged circles around their bed, unable to stop moving, refusing to be touched.

You can't help her, Mom said whenever she told that story. *She won't have it. Drives me crazy, but you just have to let her be.*

She was right (and how odd it must have been — how odd it still is — to mother someone like me), but I had no more control over my running reflex than I had over the color of my hair, my middle name.

Six years from now, Josh will drive me from our home in southern Kentucky to the hospital in Nashville one June morning as the sun rises over the lush hills, my contractions two minutes apart, bare feet on the dash and PJ Harvey crooning from the radio, *I think I'm a mother* . . . Labor will only become a scary kind of painful once the car stops moving and I stop walking and the nurses make me sit motionless in bed while they take my vitals.

But then my son will arrive with his own little face and his uncle's brown-black eyes and finally I will be still. I will want for nowhere but there, with him, my seven-pound mammal — anchor in my arms.

We'll move back to Texas soon after, where my daughter will be born — a second tether to my heart. She renames herself Ladybird for her entire kindergarten year. By then, we're back in Montana, the place I promised Josh we'd return to, which is also the place we'll decide to divorce. The place where he leaves us for good.

It's not that I won't want to drive through that pain, to throw my belongings in a car or a van and chase the horizon until I forget my own name. It's that my kids push me beyond my previous understanding of Ruth 1:16. I look into their faces — three years apart, same as Matthew and me — and I finally *feel* that verse.

For whither thou goest, I will go . . .

We are complete, the three of us a unit I want finally to travel *with,* not run *from,* no sight in the world worth seeing unless we see it together.

But no one could tell me, in Texas at the start of the millennium when all I want to do is run away, that the only way forward is through (slowly, and on foot).

Consider this: Your brother did die but returned to earth seven years ago, undercover. Tonight, he cried himself to sleep after his mother chastised him over a minor infraction. Stoned, with a jam jar of cheap wine in hand, you've crawled into his room to apologize and watch him breathe.

EIGHTEEN

Stuck

Texas: 2000

A MONTH OR SO AFTER our first meeting, I return to Pierre's. I've developed a theory about the breakdown over weeks of late-night research. The van has no engine trouble or cooling system trouble, which means her heart and circulatory systems are good. Starters tend to go out over time, but this malfunction was sudden, so it's likely not that. The battery was good, charged by a healthy alternator, but she didn't even try to turn over. And she wasn't out of gas. The Internet says to check the computer — an electronic black box the size of a book, the brain of the vehicle. Without the brain, all systems fail. I want to run the idea by Pierre. Perhaps I will learn a thing or two, play Daniel-san to his Mr. Miyagi.

The heat has lifted at last, and I drive the truck (just home from Frank's) half thinking my French mechanic a figment of my imagination. But the clusters of abandoned cars appear again, marking the way. Pierre emerges from his house as I park. He looks wary, and I realize he doesn't recognize the Ford. His shoulders relax when he sees me.

"It is you, my friend." He grabs my hand, holding it for a moment in both of his.

Friend. We are friends.

He rolls us some cigarettes and we smoke on the steps of his porch. I finally ask about the van. We approach her together, and I pause to open the door of a navy Squareback, the white vinyl interior a memory incarnate: *Matthew.*

"We used to have one of these," I tell Pierre. "When I was growing up. Same color. A red one after that."

"Someone traded me a Bug and two Squarebacks for a Peugeot. You should think about a Peugeot."

I smile and shake my head no as we face the van.

"Yours is not bad for a Volkswagen," he begins, resting a hand on the rearview mirror. I take his semi-praise as a sign that I have passed some mysterious test. As if the two of us — Pierre and I — are in this together.

"The problem is electrical. The engine, like I said, not so bad."

"It was recently rebuilt."

Pierre shrugs. "I sneef around a little more. You come back."

"I did some research and I think it might be the computer." My armchair diagnosis sends Pierre reeling.

"A computer? It could be a thousand things wrong. One thousand!" He scowls in a way that lets me know I have stepped on his toes, so to speak. Pissed in his barn. Attempted to steal his thunder.

"Just a thought," I say, feeling stupid for playing mechanic. "I read some stuff online, you know, trying to figure it out."

"Computer is an expensive part. There are simpler things. I will know more in a week. In the meantime, you have this truck, yes?"

"I do."

"How did you get such a big American vehicle? A gas guzzler, they call them. But built to last."

I find his reverence for the truck touching. Ford F-150s are the best-selling trucks of all time, and these seventies models were the first ones made, back when vehicles were composed of metal instead of fiberglass and plastic. I respect the truck, but I don't really know her. I am merely her caretaker.

"I inherited it from my brother." I look up at the sky — a recent trick I've mastered for keeping tears contained. The right eye is the problem. It leaks uncontrollably. I've learned to comfort people by claiming allergies — a legitimate ailment anytime of year in Texas.

"I see." Pierre examines my face.

"Got his dog, too. Needed the truck to bring the dog back from Georgia."

"How long?"

"A month or two. Just got it fixed."

He puts a hand on my back. "Next week then. After I sniff around some more."

I spark up the throaty Cleveland V6 and turn onto the highway, headed away from home. I've decided to visit a bar called the Devil's Backbone, where Neil has taken a job. It is usually empty, save for the tarantulas that gather near the garbage cans. It has a free shuffleboard table, one of the few games I enjoy. But mostly I want to sit near another friend and not talk. I want to not talk about my dead brother, my injured marriage, and the fact that I have no dreams for the future. I spend my time knee-deep in memory, struggling against this godforsaken place where I am stuck.

It ain't fun no more.

As the highway climbs the same hills where Lyndon B. Johnson grew up, the lights of the Ford begin to cut out. The blue of dusk still clings to sky. For a moment, I suspect my poor night vision is the problem, but each time I move the wheel, the lights extinguish until I right it. First the horn, now the lights. Even people I pay can't fix my mechanical problems. I turn back toward town.

Things are just as glitchy on the homefront. Josh isn't sleeping, and I am. I'm not writing, but he is. He's taken it up to pass the long nights.

"You can't be a writer," I tell him. "You're a musician."

"But I left my band. I can be both. What's the big deal?"

"Michael Dorris and Louise Erdrich."

Delp, my writing teacher at Interlochen, always cautioned us against mating with our own kind. The only exception to this rule, he conceded, was the partnership of Michael Dorris and Louise Erdrich, who was one of my favorite writers at the time. In 1997, years after I'd left Interlochen, Dorris committed suicide. I read he was under investigation for child abuse, leaving no exception to the rule: a writer shouldn't marry a writer.

I had spent so much of my life feeling like an outcast when I desperately wanted to be a light as bright as Matthew, Mom, or Josh. I didn't want to spend my days with a brooding golem like me, always watching, harvesting darkness from the lives of others to use as bricks in some absurd castle of words. The sparks between us are now fueled by resentment instead of attraction — a negative charge. It unnerves me to watch Josh gaining this drive I've just lost. It's a crappy way to feel about the person you vowed to love and support, and I have no clue how to fix it.

That night before sleep, I ask my Matthew to give me a sign if I should stay in my marriage or not. I whisper the question out loud, like a prayer. At three in the morning, the truck begins to blare her horn. She's parked in the drive, her hood a half-dozen feet from the bedroom window. The honking jars me out of sleep like a wake-up call from the grave. Josh, just rising for his commute to Austin, runs outside with me. We lift the hood and begin disconnecting wires until the right one pulls free and the truck falls silent. Lights flip on in nearby houses.

The next day my neighbor — Hispanic, Catholic, and nearing sixty — tells me she thought it was the tornado siren. I explain about my brother's truck. She accepts my story without question.

"Oh. So your truck is haunted," she says. "What's he want?"

I have no answer.

"See, that's what you gotta figure out. No mechanic can fix a haunting. You gotta find out what your brother needs so he can move on." She smiles and makes a Vanna White gesture toward the Ford, as if to showcase valuable evidence, then gives me a hug and returns to her porch swing.

I take the truck back to Frank's that afternoon, tell them the horn is still a problem and now the lights, too. My mechanic visits are the most regular part of my new life in Texas, it seems, my vehicles refusing to accept even the most basic repairs.

During the final week of the semester, a kind professor pulls me aside. I fear she is going to question me about my writing. I am doing the work, meeting the deadlines, but my heart is as disconnected from my stories as the truck is from its horn. If I plugged in, my words would be little more than sustained screams on the page.

"How are you doing?" She touches my arm gently, as not to break something.

"All right."

She nods, eyebrows angled in sympathy. Unsure of what she wants, I continue.

"Just busy. Final papers." There is an awkward pause when we look at each other, not understanding.

"I'm asking because you've been crying through class. Every class. All semester."

I reach a hand up to wipe the damp from my cheek. "Oh, that. It's my busted eye," I tell her. I think to mention how it's been leaking since Matthew died, how I think of it as my haunted eye, but I don't want to spread any more discomfort than I already have. "I'm not crying. It's like the drain is blocked or something. I guess I sprung a leak."

The way she smiles, I can tell she only half believes me. She pushes her curls behind her shoulders and laughs as if to say, *You don't have to pretend with me.* She tells me to use my health insurance while I have it. "See an optometrist. If your eye keeps leaking like that, your cheek will get chapped. It will sting."

There are many things I'd stopped caring about since I moved to Texas: the laziness of flip-flops, dirty feet, public drunkenness, underwear (too hot), public displays of emotion, and explaining my actions (or lack of) to others. While grief guts me daily, it frees me as well. In ways, it feels good not to give a shit. But I understand the problem: a leaky eye makes people uncomfortable. My teacher uses a subtle version of one of my mother's favorite tactics: the *I don't mind but other people might.* I appreciate someone taking notice.

"I'll look into it," I tell her, my pun too sad for a laugh.

A few days later, Frank calls to tell me about an incident at the shop. "Burglary," he says, indignant. "It is a problem in this town."

I immediately picture the eight-foot security fence surrounding the garage. Everything there is under lock and key. I can't figure out why he's calling to tell me this.

"Your truck is ready. I don't think it was touched, but you will have to check."

"Check what?"

"Personal items."

I walk to the shop and go through the truck. My items and Matthew's are still inside the cab, but the corrugated steel toolbox is empty. The leather work gloves that held the shape of his hands? Gone. The tools covered in his greased fingerprints? Gone. Only the repair manual remains.

I kneel in the truck bed, the textured plastic pressing a pattern into my knees as my bad eye flows with abandon. I don't bother trying to hide the waterworks. Frank's staff can see me cry. I can tell by their averted eyes that they know something is missing, that they remember this truck belonged to my brother, and that they understand the worth of a dead man's tools but hoped I did not.

I sit on the toolbox to process this loss, studying the low December clouds for a minute or ten. Then, with a straight face and open heart, I approach the front desk. Frank has stepped away. The same worker who waited on me the first time I came here slides the bill between us.

"Pretty sure we figured out the lights. A loose wire. The horn worked fine once we connected it. Comes to fifty even this time."

"My brother's tools were stolen."

"Tools?"

"In the toolbox. He had hundreds of dollars' worth of tools. My brother."

"Didn't you lock the toolbox?"

My cheeks light up and so do his. The focus this inspires in me is like a magnifying glass in the sun, and I concentrate everything on him. He has a point, but I can tell it shames him to make it.

"I've brought this truck here three times for electrical issues that haven't been fixed. And now you were robbed and my brother's tools were stolen. This is your problem, covered by your insurance. Yes?" It is my mother's no-bullshit voice that escapes me, and I like it.

Frank appears, looks me in the eye, and nods in agreement. He takes away the bill and helps me choose replacement tools from a catalogue. The next week, I drive by and pick up the factory-new tool set — each shiny piece of metal nested in rigid foam inside a black case. This had cost Frank's forty dollars wholesale. It had cost me something far more dear.

I decide then to let the truck be. My neighbor is right: Whatever lingers in the horn and the lights has something to say that no wiring harness can censor. I drive home, lock my new tools in their steel box, and head downtown for a pint at the Showdown. I don't say anything to Tony or Neil about the theft. Instead I tell stories about my van and Pierre, describing him as my questionable French mechanic, imitating his accent as I dramatize his ongoing promise to "sneef around," part of me aware how bankrupt I am to be using him as camouflage for my hurt.

Other abnormalities reveal themselves as the weeks after Matthew's death snowball into months. On a near daily basis I find Early Times facing the corner in a sitting position, nose aimed at the ceiling, ears at full attention. He smiles, wags his tail, and stares like that for half-hour stretches. It becomes a joke between Josh and me: *There's Early talking to angels again.*

That dog glues himself to me like a rat on cheese. He sleeps at my feet — which sends my wolf dog into a lifelong depression from which she never fully recovers. I don't know what Matthew whispered to Earl from the ether between this world and that, but the message is powerful and absolute: I am his person now, and nothing interferes with that bond. I find this comforting. Validating, I suppose, that my brother trusts me with his most loved being, and that he casts Earl as my protector — a bodyguard commissioned from beyond the grave. Though Early's continuing attempts to "protect" me from my husband and two other dogs build tension in the tinderbox we call home.

On a rare evening spent alone and sober, I hear music playing in the house as I ready myself for bed. The notes rise, starting out so faint that I mistake the sound for a song in my head. As the tones gain definition and volume, I walk through each room, searching for an electronic device left on — a forgotten radio, or a Walkman triggered by a dog perhaps. Nothing. The music grows louder. I listen for an hour, finally surrendering to the fact that this sourceless sound follows me, never louder or quieter depending on my location. I go to sleep with the song playing in my head. The faint voice has the rust and angst of early Bruce Springsteen. The only lyric I can distinguish is the word *runaway*. It is no song I've ever heard before, though it sounds much like the music my father raised us on: John Prine, Johnny Cougar, Tom Waits, the Boss. Whatever the song, it is gone by morning.

Within the week, the record collection arrives from Georgia. I assumed Victor had forgotten. (I had.) By the looks of the battered boxes, he spent days packing and duct-taping the cardboard, then sent the heavy parcels the slowest, cheapest way possible (which still likely cost him the better part of a paycheck). I unpack each box carefully, rearrange the living room around three full shelves of vinyl. The records feel a bit like guests in the house. Company.

Matthew starts to occupy my dreams. Always the same dream with subtle variations: We sit in my parents' basement, side by side, inspecting the carpet beneath our feet. Voices rise and fall overhead: Aunt Lisa's laugh loud and rough from a life spent smoking, my mother joining in. A gathering has begun. The floor joists creak under the weight of those who have loved us since the moment we entered this world. Matthew starts smiling. He has missed us. He wants to head upstairs and join the party. Then I have to tell him. Every time, every dream, that he's dead.

When Matthew and I were growing up, my father had dreams that predicted each of our broken bones (a collarbone and an arm for Matthew, a leg for me). We soon learned that when Dad said *I just had a feeling* in relation to some vague warning, it meant he'd had one of those dreams. The night Josh and I spent in Trinidad, Colorado, on the drive from Montana to Texas, I dreamed my brother's death — a dream so real I woke choking on my own sobs. When I calmed down, I called my parents to tell them about the dream, but I didn't call Matthew. I didn't even have his number. We all thought he was doing better, and I didn't want to shame him with my worry. But my dream was one of *those* dreams. I'd *just had a feeling.*

Though my postmortem dreams with Matthew aren't foresight, they aren't normal dreams either. They are visitations. Communication lines that stretch beyond the edges of the known universe. My brother, or what's left of him, finds me here. Delivering the news of his death to him rends my heart. Each time I wake up gasping for air, as if surfacing from deep waters.

> *Consider this: Your brother shot himself dead one blank-skyed Sunday, and, for reasons you can't recall but trust like brick and mortar, it was no one's fault but yours.*

Instead of doing a thorough search for an experienced eye doctor, I choose the place closest to home that accepts my health insurance. With the truck haunted, the Honda up in Austin with Josh more often than not, and the van gone to live on Pierre's farm, I frequent establishments only within walking distance of our house. A light-up sign bearing the words *Eye Doctor* marks my destination in the strip mall, sandwiched between a budget shoe franchise and a Vietnamese restaurant. Inside the receptionist greets me, pushes a stack of papers my way, and asks if I need a contact lens prescription along with my glasses prescription.

"No prescriptions," I tell her. "I'm here about a leaky eye."

Her smile releases like a rubber band. "A leaky eye?"

"A leaky eye," I repeat, pointing to it with my finger to improve our communication.

A half-hour later, I'm reclined in the windowless exam room. A doctor in his mid-twenties invites me to call him Jimmy. He wears a kind of Texas uniform: a floral print shirt, shorts, and river sandals. Jimmy extends a clammy hand.

"What happened to your eye?" He asks, reading the secretary's sticky note.

"It just leaks."

"I see." His face tenses up as if he suspects I've come in search of Lortabs or Darvoset. He rolls up closer on his wheeled stool and shines a pen light into my right eye in a way so sudden and awkward that I feel instant sympathy for all his lovers, past, present, and future.

"So nothing happened? Nothing at all?"

"My brother died a few months ago. I've cried a lot, and now my right eye won't stop."

"I see."

I make a mental note of the irony behind my eye doctor's chosen listener noise: *I see.*

Jimmy takes me through five minutes of light shining and chart reading. At the end, he shuffles my paperwork three times, rolls around the room twice, then clears his throat.

"Well, I'd say you have a blocked tear duct in the right eye."

"Blocked how?"

"I don't know," he says. "Foreign matter. An injury. Excessive use."

"Excessive use?" I say. "Like crying?"

"Yes," he says, "like crying."

There is an awkward pause between us. I have cried my right eyehole shut.

"I can irrigate." Jimmy says. "I'll use a syringe with a needle on the end. The needle will go into the corner of your eye and I'll flush the duct with water."

I stare hard at him for a moment to see if he's fucking with me.

"I think a ten-gauge is good. By the look of your duct."

It occurs to me that there's no way a healthy person with the full range of human emotions intact would let Jimmy try to penetrate their duct, but I do. The nights are growing close to cold now, and I worry about my cheek getting chapped.

Jimmy goes through two large needles, each attached to a syringe. He bungles the procedure, confesses it's the first time he's attempted such a thing, and apologizes as I leave.

Later, over beers at the Showdown, I notice my leaky eye isn't leaking anymore. Not because Jimmy fixed it the way he intended. Perhaps he simply jostled it enough to loosen whatever had been stuck. Either way, it is the first thing in my Texas life to get broken and healed.

Consider this: Your brother did die and so was there in spirit to hold your cousin Katie's hand — the one still attached to her body — two Memorial Days back, after the fatal motorcycle accident one Sunday in Binghamton, New York.

The colder Texas gets, the more I sleep. Though cold, like happiness, exists now on a revised relativity chart. Cold in Montana meant risking frostbite while walking home from the bar. Cold in Texas means the air conditioning stays off all day. Really cold means the heat kicks on, smelling of dust and disuse. Holidays, nights out, school events all pass at a distance, shadows and shapes and faces masked by an unbreakable fog. The things that come in clearest are the tangibles I hold close: my favorite pillow (extra flat), the ivory lace-weight yarn I knit with, my stack of mix tapes, the records, and the dogs who warm my feet. Even more real, perhaps, is the seamless tapestry of dreams woven by my unconscious.

Matthew continues to show up, the scene the same each time: Him sitting next to me on our parents' downstairs sofa — the place where I last saw him — wearing his black leather Harley cap and green hooded sweatshirt. My first feeling always is pure joy over his presence. The more I dream the dream, the more I am able to manipulate it the same way, as a kid, I used to fly away from *T. rexes* in my nightmares. I stretch out the first part of every visit to absorb the light of his presence. His energy. The remnants of his being. I commit his expressions and mannerisms to memory, noticing the way he holds one hand with the other, fingers fidgeting, or the way he glances sideways, moving only his eyes, when I've said something that interests him. We make small talk, crack jokes. Sometimes he asks about Texas, like we're catching up after a normal gap between visits. He asks about the weather, about lightning and thunderstorms.

No matter how lucid my dreaming, eventually the laughter interrupts us, barreling out of our relatives as they gather upstairs. He smiles and begins to get up. I catch his arm, and deliver the worst kind of news.

You can't. You're dead.

The moment I say it, his face changes as he remembers what he's done. He lowers his head to his hands and fades away. It's an injury I inflict on him again and again.

This Sisyphean reckoning reminds me of the first time I took acid. I was fifteen, at Interlochen, and my friend sat on my glasses early on in our trip. The broken spectacles bothered me, so we put them in a drawer to keep them out of sight. They were expensive, and I was so severely nearsighted that I couldn't function with-out them. What would I tell my parents if I needed a new pair? Ev-ery half-hour or so through the night-long journey, I'd open that drawer, pick up the frames, and discover all over again that they were, in fact, bent beyond repair. In the same way, I must tell my brother again and again that he is dead. Though I am grateful each time to see him, to sit next to him, the words I must deliver pull stitches loose inside me.

In other dreams I pillage houses that aren't mine, searching for a new home, some place to set down roots. The houses are all old — many of them variations of my great-grandparents' house, and some versions of our house on California Street, near the ceme-tery. The rest are stranger's houses, abandoned, as if a half-cen-tury ago the inhabitants simply vanished in their tracks, leaving tables set for dinner and linens on the line. No matter how much I dust and unpack, I can't settle. I'm called away by the sounds of a distant altercation, or the house disintegrates, leaving me to wan-der the shapeless black of the night sky: a ghost in someone else's dream, perhaps, exorcised.

Consider this: You mother didn't drink, so your brother didn't drink, but you did. You shot yourself the summer before you turned thirty and your brother never recovered. He sits at home tonight, alone in a cast-off easy chair with a fat blue heeler at his feet, star-ing at a picture of the Volaré and dreaming you back to life.

NINETEEN

Econoline

Port Aransas, Texas: 2001

*J*OSH AND I SPEND VALENTINE'S DAY of 2001 curled up on our couch in San Marcos, watching a documentary about the rise and fall of Tammy Faye Bakker, the wife of evangelist Jim Bakker, best known for her excessive eye makeup. I enjoy it the same way I enjoy the late work of Bette Davis: my fear and fascination deliciously intertwined. This, I think, must be how my brother felt about and Rog and Dewey, Brad Atkins, Victor, felons, bikers, and the many marginal characters who enjoyed the light of his admiration.

Though less than six months have passed since Matthew's death, some things have begun to settle. Bush finagles his way into the White House, which means he'll be leaving the state of Texas, at least. As the economy tanks, little startup dot-coms like the one Josh worked for in Austin vanish at an alarming rate. His is no exception. Through a series of lucky events, he lands himself a full-time job with benefits at a computer company. It comes with regular hours, a real wage, and health insurance. He starts sleeping a little better, and I start learning how to let myself laugh again.

We're over halfway through the story of Tammy Faye when the phone rings. Josh pauses the show and we stare at each other, my legs draped over his, the phone going off like an alarm. It is midnight and I flash back to that night in August when we were watching *The X-Files* and got the call about Matthew.

It could be my mother this time, I think, picturing her body limp at the bottom of the staircase, my brother a ghost beside her.

"I'll get it," I say. And I do.

My father tells me Papaw has died of a heart attack while vacationing with Mamaw in Port Aransas, Texas. After sixty years of marriage, she's alone. On Valentine's.

I look at Josh, who's following along. "We'll need directions," I say, "and an address."

With the truck still haunted and the van on sabbatical at Pierre's, we drive Mom's Honda through the moonless February night — south to San Antonio, then east toward the gulf. I recall in those wee hours my first trip to the ocean, the summer Mamaw and Papaw took me to Florida in the New Yorker. And before that, my trips to their house each July, when Mamaw taught me to crochet — a habit that soothes me when driving isn't possible. I was four when she first handed me a ball of orange yarn. I trapped it in my lap as I sat cross-legged on the couch. She showed me how to hold the yarn in one hand and the crochet hook in the other, looping, hooking, looping, hooking. Once I got the rhythm of it, she went on with her chores while I sat and crocheted. Time suspended as I hooked and wrapped, hooked and wrapped. The rows built up, the early stitches loose and gangly compared to the newer ones.

Mamaw stopped her housework to inspect what I'd decided was the beginnings of a hunting scarf.

"Not bad," she said, taking the hook from my hands.

I watched without protest as she unraveled each stitch, rewound the yarn, and dropped it back in my lap.

"But not good enough yet," she said. "Start over. Do better."

I didn't complain because I could see with my own eyes that she was right. I made a little knot, tightened it around the hook like a noose, and began to rebuild—each stitch a touch better than the last.

Consider this: On the drive from Montana to Texas, you powered on through Colorado and fell asleep at the wheel in New Mexico, where you stayed up all night in the ER with the single waking dream: lucky to be alive, lucky to be alive.

By four in the morning, we've found the vacation complex where my grandparents winter. The quiet, two-story motel looks like something out of a Hitchcock movie. In the brightening light of morning, we ascend steps covered in artificial turf, searching for my grandmother's room on the second floor.

Through an open door, I see her sitting alone on a couch, staring at her hands, painfully idle. Her hair forms the brown helmet she wore in my youth—a look crafted with fat rollers worn under a scarf overnight. Though some gray cuts through the dark brown, she looks more the same than I expected. Before I form words she finds me.

"Missy."

The sound of that name makes my bones hum. No one has said it since Matthew.

She makes us watery coffee and tells us the story as the sun comes up.

"I could tell his heart was bothering him because he'd been taking so much nitroglycerin. I told him to watch it. I *told* him." She wags a finger in the air, chastising his ghost. Her throat catches on a sob. "He went fishing in the afternoon then came home for dinner. I said, 'Benny, stay in and rest,' but he didn't listen. He left for the poker game and never made it. They found him on the stairs.

His heart just quit." She lifts her hands in disbelief, perhaps, that a life can be so suddenly extinguished.

By midday, we're knee-deep in funeral arrangements, travel reservations, and an elaborate plan to get her Ford Econoline van back to Indiana. It is a wise choice of vehicles for a pair of snowbirds. Like my van, the backseat folds into a bed. Curtains close for privacy, and the front two seats swivel around to face a small table. Recognition takes the edge off my envy — my grandparents and I have similar taste in automobiles.

Over the phone, Dad and I develop this travel algebra: Papaw's body will be flown home, Mamaw will fly out of Houston (her first air travel in thirty years), and my uncle by marriage (who happens to be visiting his family in West Texas) will meet us at the Houston airport to drive the Econoline home. Josh will drive the Honda back from Port Aransas so he won't miss a day at his new job; I will take the bus from Houston to San Marcos. Mamaw fights to ride the whole way to Indiana in her van, but my father impresses upon her in his always-gentle way that they'll need her sooner rather than later, to help with the arrangements.

In the afternoon, Josh bids us goodbye. Mamaw and I sit on the couch. I'm about to suggest a nap when a shirtless man in military-issue glasses leans through the open window, a Gomer Pyle grin stretched from ear to ear.

He gives a little wave. I wave back.

"It's the preacher." Mamaw smooths her hair. "I called him yesterday. Before you got here."

"Howdy do." The preacher tips his imaginary hat then ducks to clear the doorway. Without irony, he sports an eighties tank-top with armholes cut deep enough to expose a few ribs, a pair of too-small athletic shorts, and a light coating of sweat. It appears he has taken a break from mowing the lawn. He's about Matthew's age, I'd guess. He wipes his hand on his shorts before extending it.

"Nice to meet you," I say.

"Call me Gary." He is an awkward kind of handsome, like a young Great Dane.

"Eunice." He takes my grandmother's hands. "Tell me what happened."

She recalls the story, moving slowly over each detail as if to absorb it.

"I shouldn't be blubbering like this," Mamaw says. "Missy lost her brother last summer. My grandson. He shot himself."

Gary and Mamaw both shift their attention to me.

"I'm so sorry for your loss," Gary says, a phrase that used to irritate me but that I've come to recognize as a sign of good intentions.

"Was it a suicide?" Mamaw asks.

I know it is not an easy question for her. My parents must not be telling others the straight story because they can't accept it themselves. I look at my grandmother before I speak. I can tell that she does and does not want to know.

"It was something he wouldn't have done if he'd been sober," I say. "But he did it. He put the gun to his head and pulled the trigger."

The pastor reaches toward me, but Mamaw is between us and collapses crying into both of our arms. Gary tells us about his own struggle with depression and drinking.

"The Lord is there to hold and to heal people who suffer from all illness," he says. And then, taking my hand in his, "That means the Lord is with your brother, too, helping him heal."

It is one of the kindest things someone has said to me in a long while, and the gift rests entirely in Gary's delivery. Though for me, it isn't about God. It's about illness usurping choice. It's about understanding how he could leave me like that.

Consider this: Your brother didn't die, because you woke up in a hotel room in Colorado six days prior, drove cross-country in record time, and tethered him to earth with bone-thin arms. You are holding him still.

The sky and ocean loom large before my grandmother and me, the horizon a faint dividing line between shades of gray. We take our shoes off, our feet leaving similar prints in the sand. We talk about Papaw. We talk about Texas and Indiana and all the blue highways in between. Then we talk about Matthew. How she watched him as a baby. How we used to pop ticks off the black dog named Bear — Matthew flicking them so the blood splattered from their distended backs. How she cut the corn off the cob for him, how I cried when she stomped on the pair of baby mice I found, how I clocked my cousin in the head with a plastic clog during a dispute about who climbed the highest in the apple tree. How that one time Matthew stepped on a rusty nail in the burned-out barn.

"How did that barn burn down, anyway?"

Her face flushes red. "The old house, the barn, and the corncrib were all built by my daddy. When I married, he gave us the land on the far side of the cornfields, where Benny built our house. But we still used the barn and the corncrib. One day I went over to burn some trash in the fire pit, and a good wind come along. The barn caught fire 'fore I could do a thing about it. All the kids watched. Your daddy, too. When Benny found out he was so mad." She's laughing and crying again, bringing up from the deep a shame older than me.

"You burned down the barn."

"I did. Benny built the new barn twenty yards away, but I never could keep the kids out of that rusty ol' foundation. My dad used to hate kids running around behind his house."

"Dad's grandpa lived in the old house? The one where Uncle Kevin lives now?"

"Oh, yes. Died there, too, 'fore you were born."

"How?"

Mamaw looks at me, confused. This is a woman who helped raise her twelve siblings when her mother ran off at the start of the Depression. A woman whose father cooked up her pet goat and served it to the family for dinner the year before her own brother died in her arms on the way to the doctor in a horse-drawn buggy.

"Shotgun," she says. "Same as your brother. Same as your great-great-grandfather."

A suicide habit running straight up the spine of my paternal line. The news hits like a baseball bat to the rib cage, and some noise from the impact escapes me.

"You didn't know?"

No. "I didn't know."

And if I didn't know, I'm pretty sure Matthew didn't either. Did he?

"Someone should have told you." She put a hand on my shoulder. "My father said he'd never turn sixty. When we celebrated his sixty-first birthday, I relaxed about it. Then just days after, he shot himself in the head. His father, who was my grandfather, got put away in the Indiana State mental hospital. He couldn't get a gun in there I s'pose but he managed to hang himself from a doorknob with a shoelace."

A shoelace. She pauses and touches her neck, her eyes seeing faces long gone.

"I always worried about Matthew, but I hoped those things were behind us." Her face shifts, and she laughs as she looks at me. "I never worried about you, though. I knew you'd leave us, in a good way. You were so strong, so bright, pretty as your mama and headstrong like I never seen. Alls we had to do was stand back and let you go."

She is talking about me? Strong? And bright?

She gives me a hug.

Seashells press into the soles of my feet as they sink into sand.

She is talking about me.

Consider this: Your brother did die but sixteen years later you receive a surprise email from Danny, an antiques dealer from Indianapolis whose biological father is your father. Danny, your Other Brother, has hair the color of your son's and a record collection Matthew would adore.

We set out for Houston before sunrise. I drive the Econoline to the airport, where Mamaw will board a flight to Indiana. It gives me great pleasure to steer her toward her husband the way she once herded me to KMart, church, Florida, and back.

"You know what Benny would tell us," Mamaw says.

"Of course. *Sit back and enjoy the ride.* Even if it meant we had to pee in a potato-chip can."

These are, in fact, the only words I truly remember my grandfather delivering.

We have a good laugh-cry together.

Though I don't make it to the funeral, Dad tells me later, "Your Mamaw bragged about you to everyone. She kept saying, 'My granddaughter Missy came to help me. She bought my plane ticket, packed my van, and drove me to the airport. That girl knows where she's going, and she just goes there.'"

TWENTY

Repair

Texas: 2001

*T*HE SPRING AFTER THE BREAKDOWN I finally have the van towed back to the house. I haven't been to see Pierre since last fall. He claims to have sniffed around, but he never diagnosed — let alone fixed — any part of her. Though I didn't find a mechanic in Pierre, I did find a friend and a mentor of sorts. His automotive graveyard showed me what giving up looks like, and I couldn't do that, not to myself or to my ride.

When the van arrives, I throw on Matthew's old green sweatshirt, the one he wears in my dreams, and grab the new tool set out of the Ford. As I open the driver's door, the scent of dust, petroleum, loose tobacco, and sunbaked dashboard envelops me, and I remember the only other time I worked on her was the last time I ever talked to my brother. It was not quite a year ago — June of 2000, as we readied ourselves for the move from Missoula to Texas. In preparation for the trip, I attempted an oil change on the Vanagon by myself for the first time ever. I got out my manual, *How to Keep Your Volkswagen Alive,* and cracked the spine so the page with the oil-change instructions rested open on the ground.

I was in the process of trying to fit the socket wrench on the drain plug when Matthew called — an event rare as a thunderstorm in Montana.

"Mom says you're moving to Texas." I could hear the smile in his voice.

"I guess so. Where are you?"

I heard an echo as he spoke. "I'm in prison, but don't worry. I'm here for training, not a crime."

I'd forgotten what Mom told me: that Victor had landed Matthew a job at the dump supervising what he and Chrissie Hynde called "the chain gang." In order to supervise them, Matthew and Victor had to become official prison guards. The training happened during a solid month spent on the inside.

"How long you been there?"

"Two weeks. Two more to go."

I didn't say it, but I knew what that meant: two weeks sober, at least. Two more in the can unless he left — a longer sober stretch than he'd had, I guessed, since he became a teenager. As he drew in a breath and let it out, I sensed some animal part of him pacing the corners of his skull, thirsty.

He told me how Early ran away just before the prison stint. The dog ended up at the University of Georgia animal clinic, returned only after someone saw his distinguished mug shot on a Wanted poster my brother plastered alongside band flyers all over town. He told me how much Early liked eating rotten food at the dump. They fed him a dozen stale donuts, he said, then watched him eat a rotten cheesecake. He said Earl found a dead turkey at the dump — not a store-bought bird but one with head and feathers still intact. Matthew had thrown the carcass in the back of his new red truck and left it there, under debris, checking its state of decomposition from time to time. The story was bizarre to the point of alarm, but he'd always been the kid who got too close to dead things.

"It's more boring than you'd think on the inside, but that's okay. I prolly already read every book in the library. But I'm being real good to everyone here so they remember that if I ever come back under different circumstances." He laughed, and the sound was no less infectious for having traveled from Georgia to Montana along the wire that joined us.

I told him about feeling like Lucille Ball trying to change the oil on the Vanagon, and we laughed together.

Finally, I spilled the surprise I'd been saving: the new tattoo on my arm — a half-sleeve piece in bright colors with the number seventeen at the center (the day of my birth and my wedding) and a pair of birds pulling a banner holding the words *Made in Indiana*.

"Can't wait to see it," he said.

"You should come visit."

The line went quiet — him unable to commit to a visit because he had no faith in his sobriety, or his longevity, I guess. I wanted to give him something to show my support for the struggle we never talked about, so I made a note to send some books to him in the prison: two Jim Harrisons and a Bukowski. He devoured them in days, I know.

Then, in the moment when we usually said goodbye, Matthew said this: "Miss, I just wanted to call and say I love you. Okay?"

His voice came in clear as mountain runoff. For a moment, he was all the way there with me.

"I love you, too," I said.

And he hung up the line.

I struggled with the oil plug for another five minutes and finally decided to top off the oil and call it good. There would be time, I was sure, to learn how to care for the van. Time to anchor my marriage. Time to see my brother and find all the right words.

The longer the van sat at Pierre's, the more I sensed her time passing, slipping away for good. So I kept researching, even after

Pierre dismissed my theory about the computer. Using my manual, I walked through every issue that might have caused her sudden death. All signs pointed still to the computer.

To help me investigate further, I ordered the more technical manual — the Bentley, which is specific to Vanagons. I might not need it, but I want to be prepared, to give us both a real chance. The electrical diagrams are complex as the human vascular system — wires color-coded and crossing, one vein after another. I take a deep breath, ready to start.

Please find me where you know I need to be.

I begin with the first step in the troubleshooting sequence: turn the key. Nothing, as I expected. Next, I spin the passenger's seat around to face the rear and slide it backwards to access the oddly placed battery compartment. The battery tests well, so I check that off the list of suspects. I check the starter and alternator off the list as well because of the instant and complete nature of the failure. (Those components usually grind and protest before surrendering.) Which leaves me to test the part that's been talking to me all along: the computer. It's the brain of the vehicle, an information holder that sends signals to various components to tell them when and how to do their job. If the computer goes, no signals get sent. All operations cease.

When I called a salvage yard outside of San Antonio, they asked me repeatedly if I was sure I knew what I wanted. I was.

"It has to be a Digifant computer, from an 'eighty-three point five or an 'eighty-four. Not a Digijet."

They laughed at me. "An 'eighty-three point five?"

"Yes. Volkswagen made a half-year model in 'eighty-three. Main thing is it has to be a Digifant."

They sent me a Digijet. I sent it back and finally received a Digifant. I hold it in my hand now, and it seems such a simple thing, the size and shape of a VHS tape.

I just had a feeling . . .

I open the back hatch to access the engine. As I unscrew the mounts for the old computer, something catches my peripheral vision: tiny fire ants crawling along the black rubber of the hatch seal. I prod the seal and ants pour out of a hole in the rubber. She's infested. I'm an organic sort of girl, but Texas has driven me to drastic measures for fortifying the house against tree roaches, scorpions, and black widows. Even fire ants will crawl up a pier-and-beam foundation and into a house to save themselves from floodwaters. I find some toxic bug killer and spray the rubber carefully, watching the ants squirm then be still. They flow out in waves until at last a fire ant queen works her way through the hole. She is bigger than I'd imagined, dangerously waspish with her amber exoskeleton and angled wings. She writhes, stuck in that gray area between life and death. I see in her struggle the past half-year of my life, stuck somewhere between atrophy and flight. Some things, however, are beyond repair. I brush her to the ground and end her suffering with the sole of my Converse.

It ain't fun no more.

I remove the old computer and plug in the new one. The job is far simpler than I'd imagined. Still, I'm nervous, trained for a lifetime to think this the kind of job only a Pierre, Frank, or Lester can handle. I pause and breathe my way through doubt, reminding myself I can hardly destroy this non-running van. She has oil. She has gas. But no spark. Swapping a computer may not fix her, but isn't going to harm her. The worse that can happen is nothing. And nothing is already the problem, leaving me nothing to lose.

Do better.

I mount the new computer and climb behind the wheel. The sleeves of Matthew's sweatshirt pushed up to my elbows in the warming day, I slip her into neutral and turn the key. *Pause. Sputter. Spark.* The *tick tick tick* (pause) *tick tick tick* of the engine reviving causes the neighbors to look up from their gardening. My heart combusts along with the cylinders. Stunned by my good fortune, I feather the pedal until her beat holds steady, then pull the parking brake, run out to close the hatch, and take her on a spin around the neighborhood.

Okay then.

I can tell the fuel line is clogged, likely from months spent dormant. She doesn't want to go over thirty. We weave through the streets, working out the kinks. I forgot how you have to put a little muscle into turning the oversize steering wheel, how this van rides high and smooth as a space ship. I forgot how the world looks better from up here. I do a couple victory laps around the neighborhood, test her bright little horn, even, and bring her home.

Consider this: Your brother put a bullet through his skull one slow, sticky Sunday in the Athens, Georgia, landfill, and it was no one's fault at all.

Some nights, Matthew walks with me through the halls of the Holiday Inn I dreamed of way back in Colorado, the rooms stacked in floors around an atrium. On these journeys, we're late, searching together for a family gathering. Matthew shoves his hands in pockets as he walks beside me, a smile on his face and his body buoyed by excitement — he has missed everyone so much. But then I tell him. *You're dead, you can't . . .* We stop in the maze of hallways, our eyes soldered to the hunter-green carpet under the weight of my devastating words. The dream ends here. I either wake or fall into a black sleep below dreams. But I never walk away. I never leave him. I can't.

I have two broken legs . . .

I don't recall exactly when the dreams end, but sometime before the start of our second Texas summer, they do. Matthew simply disappears from the edges of my world, having moved on, at last, to whatever comes next. Every now and then, when I come across an old picture of him smiling sparkly-eyed while riding on the back of a garbage truck, or the eight-year-old him running military-style through the neighborhood with a BB gun in hand, wearing the same expression I see so often these days on my own son's face — my chest seizes up like an overworked engine.

Mama.

I take a breath. I let go all over again. (I am letting go now.)

Consider this: You never _____ and he never _____ so we didn't _____ and nothing ever happened at all.

Trooper

Montana: July 2014

*J*ULY AGAIN IN MONTANA, and my son and I attempt to
fix our camper van while his five-year-old sister naps in the
house. He is eight, obsessed with drawing and World War II, and
is excited beyond words that we are working on the van together.

"Hey, buddy, can you grab me two pencils?"

"Are you going to write something?"

"No, we're going to use them to fix Trooper. Go get them and I'll
show you."

People say the kids are Matthew and me all over again, but they
demonstrate on a regular basis a kindness toward each other that
Matthew and I never possessed. Perhaps this closeness is a side effect of the instability that marked their earliest days. My son was
born in Nashville, though we were residents of Kentucky at the
time. His sister is a bona fide Texan. Now we live in Missoula, the
forever-home we coasted into after failed attempts to put down
roots in Michigan and Indiana. In the midst of this chaos, home became not a location but anywhere the three of us landed, together.

I rest underneath the van and soon my son's feet flip-flop toward me. He kneels down, offering a pair of his pencils.

"Can I have these back? They're my favorites."

"They're going to smell like gas."

"But I really, really like these ones."

"I'll buy you a couple new pencils, okay?"

He brushes his shoulder-length hair out of his face, his brow fierce with concern. He is a collector, and sharing pains him.

"It's for Trooper, buddy."

"Okay then."

I bought this van months after becoming a single parent. I realized that the kids had never been camping (due in large part to all those cross-country moves). She's a 1984, same as my first van, only a Westfalia. She has a kitchen and a pop-top and sleeps four. She's my first white vehicle, which put me off initially since most of the vehicles in my life have been brown. But her noncolor has since become part of her charm. I bought her in an eBay auction — a precarious decision at best — then caught a ride to Casper, Wyoming, to drive her home. I suggested we name her Casper, but the moment my son first saw her he said she looked like a storm trooper from Star Wars. I watched him explore the van with his sister, age two at the time, turning knobs in the kitchen — their father several states away indefinitely — and the ghost of my state trooper grandfather hovering nearby. The name seemed to fit: a Trooper for a couple of troopers.

Fixing the computer on my old van did not fix me, or fix my grief. It was not like the end of a Hallmark movie, where some glacial thing inside me melted into the warm, Caribbean sea of my future. What I found in that moment is the seed of a persistence I would need in the years to come. Each time it was tested, my resolve grew.

Josh and I were in and out of Texas until 2010. By that time, all of the old cars had left us.

A couple years after I fixed her, I sold my first van to Tony

Chapa, the friend who'd left her stranded in the taco shop parking lot in San Marcos. Though I did resurrect her, she suffered a handful of other problems caused by sitting idle for so long at Pierre's. I was underpaid and overworked and could no longer justify dedicating time and money to healing a van with no air conditioning in the heat of the South. Tony fixed her up with his father's help and took her all over Mexico, abandoning her finally in Belize. There could be no better ending for a van of her kind. I like to imagine her living there still, tires years flat, a makeshift home for squatters, or a bohemian chicken coop in someone's backyard.

Tony Chapa played a role in the demise of the truck, as well. A few years after he'd borrowed the van, Chapa moved again. He asked Josh if he could use the truck while I was at work one day. Josh agreed, and Chapa ran that Ford all over Austin in the August heat. When Josh drove it to the store later in the day, the giant six-cylinder Cleveland engine seized, drained of oil.

Dad couldn't let the Ford go. He paid to have the engine rebuilt. Josh and I then delivered the rehabilitated truck to him in Indiana. Mom hated the sight of it parked on the street. To have an ungaraged vehicle, in her line of thinking, is low class, and my father felt guilty about not using it. It was a relic. A thing of symbolic value. An object without purpose, which is a hefty kind of sadness. After a year or so, Dad struck a deal with Ralph, the family's longtime pool man. Ralph's son, Ricky, would buy the truck on a payment plan. Ricky was fresh out of prison for maybe the third time. Dad saw the truck all over town, increasingly worn down, and Ricky stopped making payments. Dad eventually repo-ed the truck using a spare key. Soon after, Ricky took a crowbar to it in the night, smashing that cherry paint job, steel trim, headlights, and windshield to high heaven. The truck was totaled, and my father did away with it, which was as hard on his heart as incinerating his son's body.

Mom's Honda never made it out of Texas. The rusted radiator blew a hole during one of Josh's highway commutes. Because of a busted stereo, he'd taken to listening to music on headphones as he drove. Passersby waved at him, and he waved back. By the time he noticed in the rearview the giant plume trailing him, it was too late. He pulled off the upper ramp of I-35 in Austin and coasted into a parking space as the engine seized. A Honda with only 111,000 miles. She was just getting started.

In 2006, my son was born and I worked as the breadwinner while Josh earned his second master's degree. Teaching, child-rearing, mowing the lawn, and doing the laundry took all my energy — there was no time to write. Days before Thanksgiving of 2008, I found out I was pregnant with our second child — one of the happiest, most ill-timed surprises of my life. It was the same week the company I worked for shut down entirely, leaving me pregnant and unemployed with a toddler and a graduate student at home, the home where our daughter was born in July of 2009.

The next January, my mother suffered a life-threatening ARI (the abbreviation for an alcohol-related injury). She barely survived an emergency brain surgery in which a blood vessel burst moments after doctors removed a piece of her skull. I flew up with my baby and toddler to help out for a month. She came home and kept drinking from wine bottles hidden in various parts of the house. I did wound care on my mother's shaved head, nursed my infant, and played Legos with my son, while secretly organizing an intervention that forced my mother into the first of multiple rehab stints. After what happened to Matthew, I had to try. I owed it to her to stand up and say the hard thing, the true thing, a thing I knew would hurt.

She came home from rehab, went back to drinking, and by the end of the year, the one brain surgery turned into five brain surgeries because her skull would not heal.

By spring of 2010, Josh and I became transients with a one-year-old and a four-year-old in tow. The economy had tanked, taking with it my job and his job prospects. We ended our lease in Austin and house-sat for friends through summer. I landed a fall teaching gig back at Interlochen. Then, with no place to go, we moved in to my parents' basement. My mother continued drinking, stumbling on the stairs in front of the kids — the same stairs where she'd acquired her ARI.

One night, I pulled her out of her running car, parked in the garage, door closed. (It's the same 1999 Honda CRV she drives today.) The next day, she returned to rehab.

In spring, Josh's short stories started winning awards. He began picking up work in the advertising world, and I started landing some freelance editing jobs. With no home to go home to and some cash in our pockets, we returned to Missoula. Shortly after that, he left to attend a writing residency in Pennsylvania while I stayed back with the kids. By fall of 2011, we decided to divorce.

I used to blame writing for being the thing that broke us, but it was as much writing as it was the fact that we got stuck owning a house in 2006, and I lost my full-time job in 2008, and Josh graduated in 2009, when full-time jobs were as rare as lush gardens in the Dust Bowl. We'd been divvying up limited resources for so long that I couldn't untangle my resentments from our love. After sixteen years of near-constant proximity, I no longer knew who I was without him. *Melissa-'n'-Josh. Josh-'n'-Melissa.* The complexities of the truth still elude me, like trying to close your eyes and imagine this planet, the solar system, our galaxy — one among millions that make up the known universe. It's too much, and writer versus writer is merely one star in that vast constellation.

Josh soon sold the novel he'd written during our marriage and settled eventually in Los Angeles. He still claims one of the top ladder rungs on my heart, and it makes me happy to think that some of my drive rubbed off on the boy I met in Missoula in 1995, a funny guy who masked his big heart with a hair-trigger wit, a guy who'd never even owned a car. Under the most unlikely circumstances, we've both turned into the writers we tried so hard to be. Though he is there for our kids as a long-distance father in ways I never dreamed possible, I have raised them solo since they were two and five. Resentment is irrelevant — my gut tells me I am exactly where I am supposed to be.

"Mama," my son says, "do you believe in werewolves?" He's slid underneath the van next to me.

"I don't know. I mean, there's no evidence. They're likely made up."

A shadow eclipses his face and I can tell he's been having his own shark dreams. I think fast to clear his mental sky.

"Know what I do know for sure?"

"What?"

"You smell like poop."

He laughs hysterically, rolling on the ground as I tickle him. I catch the earthy scent of his unwashed head, a smell I will take beyond the grave if I can take anything at all.

With the repair manual nearby and a pan underneath the first fuel connection, I unscrew the clamp and pull it loose. Gas spills out in the brief moment before I can fit the pencil into the hose.

"Whoa," my son says. "What's that smell?"

"Gasoline. See how we plugged the line with your pencil?"

For reasons as complex as an Old Testament genealogy, the new pump does not attach to the old fuel filter. I cut lengths of hose to try to make the connections. He inspects the job and smiles over his contribution. "Do you like the smell of gas, Mom?"

"It gives me a headache."

"Oh. I kind of like it."

As a kid, so did I. "That's okay. Just don't smell it a lot. On purpose. It's bad for your brain."

"How is it bad?"

We continue on like that, playing twenty questions as he hands me pencils and rags and screwdrivers and wrenches. I love that my kids ask all the questions, though some of them are hard ones, like, *How'd you get those two scars on your arm, Mom?*

I got cut.

Or, *How did your brother die?*

He got shot.

I do my best to tell a truth they can handle now, though one day those answers will need to shift from passive to active in order to tell the larger truth.

I cut myself.

He shot himself.

I will tell them that they have higher odds in the genetic lottery for inheriting mood and substance disorders, so they will have to be vigilant about that. I will tell them about suicide, how we owe those we love our participation in this world, and how we owe our future selves the chance to live through those dark hours. I will promise to protect my life and theirs, and that every hour of every day for as long as the three of us live, my house and heart are open to them.

Do you miss your brother? my son once asked.

Yes, I said. *Every day.*

I tighten the last bolt and wipe the grime off my hands. Replacing the water pump is not an ending. The only thing I know for sure about this thirty-some-year-old vehicle is that she will break again and again, so we carry with us always our tools and manuals.

We rest for a moment on our backs in the shade of the van.

"Good job, fella."

He smiles, and I spy a certain gentle something in his face that reminds me of Matthew.

"Can I tell you a joke, Mom?" He has his grandfather's intuition, sensing changes in my moods before I do.

"Of course."

"Knock knock."

"Who's there?"

"Werewolf Boo."

I try not to smile before delivering the set-up line. "Werewolf Boo who?"

"Oh, don't cry, Mom, it's just a joke!"

The moment he says the words, I'm in the rear of the Square-back again, singing along to "Werewolves of London" like that day happened a heartbeat ago. I sing a few bars for my son. He smiles like now I'm the joker, his gaze a divine spotlight in which I loom as large as one of my mother's silver screen stars.

"We're fixing the car, right, Mom?"

"Yes," I tell him.

We are fixing a car. We are making a memory. And when his sister wakes, we'll go for a drive.

There is one question no one asks, though it used to hang over my days like years' worth of bad weather: *Could you have saved him?*

Yes.

I could have gone to Georgia and held him to the earth with my arms, but he would have hated it. I think he knew that my own young life was often more than I could handle back then. You can Monday-morning-quarterback the past for the rest of your days, but it never changes the score.

The irony is that surviving Matthew's death gave me the grit I would need to save us both the only way I know how: Here, in these pages. This book.

ACKNOWLEDGMENTS

Many thanks to Vermont Studio Center, Montana Arts Council, and Interlochen Center for the Arts for helping me afford the time and space to write a first draft.

Thanks to the many readers whose encouragement and wisdom powered me on: Karen Rice, Sarah Maigin Smith, Melissa Stuart, Debbie Carney, Dalia Azim, Domenica Ruta, Jon Marc Smith, Charlotte Creekmore, and Malcolm Brooks.

To my brother's friends, for having the generosity and courage to share your Matt stories with me.

To the mentors who filled up my tank and gave me direction: Michael Delp, Chris Offutt, Tim O'Brien, and Debra Monroe.

To Amy Williams and Helen Atsma, for their superb guidance, diehard support, and uncanny ability to see the light in this book.

To Joshua Smith Henderson — my once-husband, forever co-parent, and constant cheerleader. You hold more heavy and light than any human I've known.

To my dad, for showing me how to find the extraordinary in the ordinary, from music to cars to people.

To my mom, for teaching me to find humor in the most unlikely places.

And to my entire wild-hearted Hoosier tribe: for loving me beyond reason, letting me go, and welcoming me back every time. You are better than I deserve.

ABOUT THE AUTHOR

Melissa Stephenson earned her B.A. in English from the University of Montana and her M.F.A. in fiction from Texas State University. Her writing has appeared in publications such as *The Rumpus,* the *Washington Post, ZYZZYVA,* and *Fourth Genre. Driven* is her first book. She lives in Missoula, Montana, with her two kids.